Just Let Me PREACH

THE BIOGRAPHY OF PAUL TASSELL

Just Let Me PREACH

THE BIOGRAPHY OF PAUL TASSELL

Nathan O. Osborne III

REGULAR BAPTIST PRESS
1300 North Meacham Road
Schaumburg, Illinois 60173-4806

JUST LET ME PREACH: The Biography of Paul Tassell
© 2002
Regular Baptist Press
Schaumburg, Illinois
1-800-727-4440

RBP5267 • ISBN: 0-87227-672-4
Printed in the United States of America.

DEDICATION

To Jill Priscilla
An adoring daughter
A beautiful wife
A caring mother

ACKNOWLEDGMENTS

This book would have been impossible without the assistance of some wonderful people.

Thanks to Norman Olson, Jonita Barram, and all the staff at Regular Baptist Press for their hard work and encouragement.

Thanks to Faith Baptist Church, especially the deacons of Faith, who allowed me extra time away to spend putting pen to paper. I would also like to thank my secretary, Georgia Taylor, for her invaluable assistance. Thank you to David and Valarie Auvil, who provided a quiet and beautiful place for me to work.

A special thank you to my brother John Osborne, who has been a mentor, constructive critic, encourager, and friend.

Thank you to Mom Tassell for her invaluable insight in the making of this book. Doris Tassell is a woman of remarkable strength and self-sacrifice who has spent her life working hand in hand with her husband and now cares for his every need with the tenderness and compassion of Christ.

And to my beloved wife, Jill, and our four children—Hannah, Nathan, Reagan, and Sarah—thank you for your patience, kindness, and love while I worked on this project. I will always be grateful to our God for the blessings of you!

CONTENTS

Foreword 9

Introduction 13

1 A Terrific Trio 17

2 Lightweight Champion of the World 29

3 Bob Jones University 35

4 Second Baptist Church, Elberton, Georgia 43

5 Doris Jaeger 49

6 Bethany Baptist Church, Galesburg, Illinois 55

7 The Crown of Rejoicing 65

8 Campus Baptist Church, Ames, Iowa 77

9 The Glory Years 83

10 Contending for the Faith 95

11 National Youth Representative 101

12 Grandview Park Baptist Church, Des Moines, Iowa . . 109

13 National Representative 117

14 The GARBC 125

15 Fifty Years a Preacher 141

16 Just Let Me Preach 159

Addendum I Debate over the Virgin Birth of Christ . . . 163

Addendum II Best-Loved Sermons Preached
by Paul Norman Tassell 177

FOREWORD

PREACHING is the priority ministry of God's servants in every generation, for God has committed His message to men for the purpose of preaching it "in season [and] out of season" (2 Timothy 4:2). The life story of Dr. Paul Norman Tassell, which you are about to read, reflects the conviction that Paul Tassell is a man consistently ready to preach the Word of God with passion, purpose, and power.

I count it an honor to write this foreword to the account of his life and ministry. You will find, as I have, that Paul Tassell, like the prophet Jeremiah, was born to preach. God's gift for preaching became evident early in Tassell's life, and that gift has been supported by many years of fruitful ministry.

My association with Dr. Tassell began through our contacts in the General Association of Regular Baptist Churches (GARBC). For many years I was simply in the audience, where he would challenge my spirit through his dynamic preaching. Then our fellowship became more personal when he ministered at the educational institutions where I was involved, and when my wife and I entertained him in our home. Dr. Paul is my friend and fellow laborer in the ministry.

Dr. Tassell has served God with dignity and distinction in a variety of ministries: pastor, Bible conference speaker, youth director of the General Association of Regular Baptist Churches, and national representative of the GARBC.

His preaching of God's Word is the hallmark of his life.

Dr. Tassell's exposition of a text has always been clear and applied with deep conviction. The listener's interest and recall have been aided by Dr. Tassell's mastery of the art of alliteration. Beyond this mastery is his ability to preach God's Word like a branding iron burning on the hearts of his listeners. His piercing blue eyes make a listener feel that the message is directed right at his heart.

Leadership that combined compassion with conviction marked Dr. Tassell's time as the national representative of the GARBC. He cared greatly about the pastors and people of our Fellowship, giving counsel and encouragement to them. At the same time, he maintained strong Biblical convictions.

Effective communication of God's Word requires that a leader or speaker be credible. He must be perceived as having high qualifications and integrity; in other words, he must be a man of character. The apostle Paul stressed the important relationship of his character to ministry when he wrote to the Thessalonian church of "how holily and justly and unblameably we behaved ourselves among you that believe" (1 Thessalonians 2:10). While no man is perfect, it is well known that Dr. Tassell has impeccable character. He has run the race well and is finishing strong.

The test of a man's true character is revealed in his personal life. My experiences with Dr. Tassell's family reveal a wife and children who love him, as well as the Lord he serves. In these later years Dr. Paul is being put through the testing fire of physical disability. However, this attack upon his body has not diminished his love for the Lord's work. He continued serving and preaching until it was no longer possible for him to do so. Perhaps because both of us have gone through physical testing, I have been more keenly aware of the way Dr. Paul demonstrates the sufficiency of God's grace in his life. I well remember his series of messages on the sovereignty of God in Job's testing, and today he is demonstrating the reality of that message in his own life.

As you read the story of the life and ministry of Dr. Paul Tassell, you will readily see that the often-repeated phrase "just let me preach" is the distinguishing mark of this man of God.

Elvin K. Mattison, Ph.D.

INTRODUCTION

DR. PAUL NORMAN TASSELL spends most of his day sitting in an electric lounge chair. His once powerful voice is now quiet. His once quick and sharp mind fades in and out of reality. His body has broken down. He is quietly preparing to step on Heaven's shore and humbly bow in the presence of his Savior and Lord, Jesus Christ.

Dr. Tassell is my father-in-law. I have the privilege of being married to his second daughter, Jill. While visiting my in-laws in their home in the summer of 1997, I asked Dad Tassell if he had ever thought about putting together a biography. The following year, after moving to Winter Haven, Florida, Dad showed up at my office door and asked, "Are you ready to write a book?" That question started an adventure that would last over two years.

Almost every week for the next eighteen months, usually on a Wednesday, I would arrive at Mom and Dad Tassell's condominium, sit at their dining room table, listen to their stories, take notes on Dad's dictation, and watch Dad's voice and body slowly deteriorate due to Parkinson's disease. Those sessions would last from one hour to three hours, depending on my schedule and Dad's strength.

Just Let Me Preach is a biography of Paul Tassell's life based on his memory and a few interviews from family members, coworkers, and people from the churches he pastored. It is not a scientific study that analyzes all the minute details or cross-references all the dates, times, and places. It is simply a book about a man called to preach the gospel of Jesus Christ. This is his story from his memory. We must realize that some of his recollections of different events might be different from the way the people in those stories remember them; however, the purpose was to write about Dr. Tassell's life from his perspective. Throughout the book are sprinkled some of my own thoughts, ideas, and opinions about an event that took place or the times in which we live and minister.

There can never be another book written like this one. Dr. Tassell's mind and mouth have been closed by an evil disease. The many hours spent interviewing and listening to him will be a treasure to me on which I will never be able to place a value. I had the privilege of knowing a man who had a clear-cut purpose in life. He knew what that purpose was when he was fourteen years old, and for fifty years he did not waver from what he knew God wanted him to do. He was called of God to preach the Bible, and that is exactly what he devoted his life to do. Dr. Tassell preached without shame, without hesitation, and without fear.

Dr. Paul Norman Tassell may have stood only five feet seven inches tall, but he packed a powerful punch in the pulpit, preaching with persuasive purpose all across this great country. That is why he wanted to title this book *Just Let Me Preach*.

In the process of writing the manuscript many people have asked me, "Why did God let this happen to Dr. Tassell?" Paul and Doris Tassell are not among those who questioned God's decision making. They have graciously submitted to the sovereign will of God and continue to praise Him for the privilege of serving Him.

> For I reckon that the sufferings of this present time are not worthy to be compared with the glory which shall be revealed in us . . . .

Because the creature itself also shall be
delivered from the bondage of corruption into
the glorious liberty of the children of God
(Romans 8:18, 21).

A Terrific Trio

*There are two kinds of women in the world: those who take
a man's strength and those who give a man strength.*

IHRE FREUNDIN

A MAN'S knowledge of women is limited. No matter how hard he tries, no matter which way he turns, no matter what words exit his mouth, a woman's mood, manner, and maneuver will be what he least expects. On the other hand, man would be utterly alone, lost in the cynical nature of his own mind, without the challenge of a loving woman.

Three women played major roles in the shaping of a faithful man through the early years of his life. Paul Norman Tassell was born during a time when the men and women of the United States were mustering their energies just to survive the Great Depression. A terrific trio of women stepped up to the plate and had an enormous impact on a boy's life—not just for a summer, or even for a year, but for a lifetime.

William Ross Wallace correctly wrote, "The hand that

rocks the cradle is the hand that rules the world."[1]

This unsung trio will never be featured in a history book. By most standards, what they accomplished in life was trivial. However, by either a small action, an encouraging word, or just by being in the right place at the right time, they influenced a young boy's life, and this influence would have national repercussions for the cause of Jesus Christ.

THE GREAT DEPRESSION

October 29, 1929, better known as Black Tuesday, was the day the American stock market came crashing down. The value of stocks and securities dropped a whopping $26 billion. Before another month would pass, the losses climbed to more than $100 billion nationwide. Businesses and banks shut down for lack of money and customers. During the next few years the United States and the rest of the world would sink into what we now call the Great Depression. Men who had once been millionaires literally stood on the street corners selling apples, hoping to earn a nickel. Bread lines formed in every city, with thousands of people looking for something to eat. In 1931, more than twenty thousand people committed suicide. The popular song of the day was "Brother, Can You Spare a Dime?" The United States had never before seen misery or poverty of that degree. In the middle of that Great Depression, Paul Norman Tassell was born on July 20, 1934.

PAUL'S FATHER, ALBERT

Paul was the second male child born to Albert and Bessie Tassell. Just ten months earlier on September 1, 1933, his older brother, Al, had been born. Someone had told Bessie that J. R. Rice said a woman couldn't get pregnant if she were nursing. J. R. and Bessie were wrong.

Albert Burton Tassell, Paul's father, was the son of Joseph and Caroline Tassell. Joseph and Caroline had come to the United States from Herne Bay, England, in 1898 to search for work and a better lifestyle in which to rear their children. Joseph was a tool and die maker. The couple settled in Toledo, Ohio. There Joseph and his wife became charter members of Emmanuel Baptist Church of Toledo. God blessed them with six children. Albert Burton was number five.

Albert Tassell was born on August 14, 1907, one year before Henry Ford introduced his Model T. Albert was a big, rawboned, burly young man. He had a mind of his own and big powerful fists. One day while Albert was at football practice for Libby High, a coach yelled at him to get his big rear end down. In a stubbornness that seems to be bred in some young folks, Albert stood up and walked away from football and high school, never to return.

PAUL'S MOTHER, BESSIE
First of the Terrific Trio

Bessie Ruth Gibson was born on January 13, 1911, in Wartrace, Tennessee, near Shelbyville. She was the youngest of four daughters born to Oscar and Betty Gibson. Bessie went to a one-room schoolhouse and made it through the sixth grade. Like most young people in those World War I years, she then went to work to try to help her family eke out a living. In 1929, when Bessie was eighteen years old, her father decided it was best to move to Toledo. Maybe there in the bigger city he could do better for his family. Six months later the stock market came crashing down.

In Toledo the Gibson family began attending
Emmanuel Baptist Church. One Sunday night after the
evening service, the young people were invited to a
"singspiration." On that particular evening someone invited
Albert Tassell to be a part of the group. That invitation
would change the course of his life. At the singspiration
Albert found himself staring into a pair of beautiful blue
eyes, which happened to belong to Bessie Gibson. The
year was 1931, and the country was sloshing around in the
muck of economic disaster. But that quandary could not
stop the power of true love. On July 1, 1931, after a lengthy
courtship of four weeks, Albert borrowed his older brother
Howard's Hudson Terraplane and secretly picked up
Bessie. They headed to Fort Wayne, Indiana, to be married
by a justice of the peace. Albert and Bessie, whom he lovingly called "Sweetie-pie," spent the next forty-two years together as husband and wife.

THE TASSELL HOUSEHOLD

In 1932, Franklin Delano Roosevelt was elected president of the United States. Albert Tassell, nicknamed
"Buster," sold insurance and boxed semiprofessionally to
make ends meet. Bessie became a quiet homemaker,
rearing the children and taking in laundry to supplement
Buster's income. Buster's parents, Joseph and Caroline,
were victims of the Depression. Joseph lost his job, and
the couple lost their home. Albert and Bessie opened
their home to the elder Tassell couple. Just a couple
months later, in July 1934, Paul Norman Tassell entered
this world.

Most children growing up in the Midwestern town of
Toledo in the midst of family and friends did not feel the

harshest effects of the Depression. The neighborhood was like family, and people watched out for one another. The Tassell family continued to attend Emmanuel Baptist Church. Dr. James T. Jeremiah was the pastor, and he preached messages that convicted the heart and stirred the soul.

PAUL BECOMES A BELIEVER

One Sunday night in August 1941, Paul had just celebrated his seventh birthday. That night Pastor Jeremiah preached a convicting gospel message. Even at that young age, Paul knew that his sin was separating him from God. He also knew that Jesus Christ had died on the cross of Calvary and shed His own blood so that he could have everlasting life. Paul tried to suppress the convicting power of the Holy Spirit.

Al and Paul shared a bedroom. In the open space at the head of the stairs stood an old-fashioned floor-model radio. On Sunday mornings the family started the day listening to M. R. De Haan's "Radio Bible Class." On Sunday nights Al and Paul were to stay in their room and quietly listen to a radio program from Detroit called "Echoes from Heaven." That particular Sunday night, as Paul listened to the radio program, the words of Pastor Jeremiah also echoed through his mind. The conviction of the Holy Spirit came in such sheer force that Paul could not hold back the tears. The burden of sin lay heavy on his heart, and he knew he was bound for Hell if he remained the way he was. His mother heard Paul's sobs and came into the room to see what was the matter. Paul fell into her arms and cried, "I'm not saved, and I'm headed to Hell." Bessie got her Bible; together mother and son knelt by the bed as she read John

3:16: "For God so loved the world, that he gave his only be-
gotten Son, that whosoever believeth in him should not
perish, but have everlasting life." Then she read 1 John
5:10–12: "He that believeth on the Son of God hath the witness in himself: he that believeth not God hath made him a
liar; because he believeth not the record that God gave of
his Son. And this is the record, that God hath given to us
eternal life, and this life is in his Son. He that hath the Son
hath life; and he that hath not the Son of God hath not life."
At that point Paul's mother directed her son to bow his
head and believe on the Lord Jesus Christ. Paul testified, "I
said I would, and I did." On that hot August night in the
quietness of his own bedroom, under the tutelage of his
faithful mother, Paul Norman Tassell became a child of
God. His sins were forgiven, and Jesus became His personal Savior. Two years later Dr. James T. Jeremiah baptized Paul, and the youth was added to the membership of
Emmanuel Baptist Church.

THE "PROPHETS" OF GOD

Both Al and Paul became Baptist preachers. Al talked
Grandpa Gibson, who was working as a truck farmer, into
giving them two orange crates that became their pulpits.
First they would coerce their sisters—Ruth Ann, Barbara,
and Caroline—into being the congregation, and then they
expanded their congregation by inviting the neighborhood
kids to join them. Al and Paul took turns leading the singing and preaching to those "wretched sinners."

One bright afternoon while their mother was in an up-
stairs bedroom napping with their three sisters, Al and
Paul decided to play a game they made up called "The
Prophets of God." Al played the part of Elijah, and Paul

played Elisha. The object was to call down fire from
Heaven. The brothers took table matches from the kitchen
and proceeded to the backyard in full view of their
mother's bedroom window. There, as prophets of old, Al
and Paul "cried out to God" to send His holy fire from the
portals of Heaven upon their sisters' baby buggy. They
struck a match, and in seconds the baby buggy was ablaze.
Realizing that they were going to have a tough time trying
to blame the fire on God, Al and Paul tried to beat out the
flames. A neighbor woman began to scream, which woke
their mother. Even though the fledgling prophets got the
fire out, they knew their dad would light an even hotter fire
upon their posteriors when he came home. Their prophecy
came true, as their earthly father set fire to their backsides
with five lashes apiece with his razor strap. He then sent
them to a cooling-off session in the bathtub. Paul later recalled concerning his dad's punishment, "Dad's discipline
was often stern, but he always ended up at the end of the
day praying with us and for us as we sat on his knee.
Lickings and love do go together."

AUNT CLARA
Second of the Terrific Trio

Aunt Clara Tassell lived just two or three blocks from
Paul's house. He often stopped at Aunt Clara's house on
the way home from school for two reasons: first, Aunt
Clara always had freshly baked cookies waiting for his eager taste buds, and second, Aunt Clara had a Victrola and a
small stack of 78 rpm records. She let Paul listen as much
as he liked. He played one particular song performed by a
southern gospel quartet over and over again—sometimes
seven or eight times in a row. Aunt Clara never became angry or ordered him to put it away. The song was "Stepping

in the Light," written by Eliza E. Hewitt and put to music by William J. Kirkpatrick. The lyrics are,

> Trying to walk in the steps of the Savior,
> Trying to follow our Savior and King;
> Shaping our lives by His blessed example,
> Happy, how happy, the songs that we bring.
>
> Pressing more closely to Him who is leading,
> When we are tempted to turn from the way;
> Trusting the arm that is strong to defend us,
> Happy, how happy, our praises each day.
>
> Walking in footsteps of gentle forbearance,
> Footsteps of faithfulness, mercy and love,
> Looking to Him for the grace freely promised,
> Happy, how happy, our journey above.
>
> Trying to walk in the steps of the Savior,
> Upward, still upward we'll follow our Guide;
> When we shall see him, "the King in his beauty,"
> Happy, how happy, our place at His side.
>
> How beautiful to walk in the steps of the Savior,
> Stepping in the light, Stepping in the light;
> How beautiful to walk in the steps of the Savior,
> Led in paths of light.

Aunt Clara often chatted with Paul about the words of that song and encouraged him to be a faithful man of God. She consistently told him how important it is for a real man to walk in the steps of the Savior. Those truths were drilled into Paul's heart and mind by a sweet aunt who had cookies, a record player, and time for a little boy. Breast cancer took Aunt Clara in 1950. At the end she weighed less than eighty pounds, but she never lost her faith in the goodness of God. Paul's testimony of Aunt Clara was that "she had a warm and radiant testimony that lightened my journey through the years."

GRANDMA TASSELL
Third of the Terrific Trio

From the very beginning, Paul Tassell had a clear, sharp mind. By the age of five he had learned how to read. Reading would become his lifeblood. It was Grandma Tassell who instilled into his soul the love of reading God's Word.

The year Paul was born, Grandma Tassell suffered a series of strokes that left her paralyzed and dependent upon the care of her family. As the years went by and the boys grew, their responsibility for their invalid grandmother increased. When Paul was five, his daily jobs included feeding Grandma her breakfast of oatmeal and reading to her from the Bible before he left for school. Her favorite book was Ephesians. In the beginning Paul read just a few lines; then he progressed to entire verses. By the time he turned seven years of age, Paul was reading complete chapters, which eventually led to his reading the whole book to his grandmother at one sitting. This practice continued until God called Grandma Tassell to Heaven.

What Grandma Tassell gave to her grandson was a deep love for the Word of God, especially the book of Ephesians. The discipline of reading the Bible and gaining strength from its life-giving words, which would sustain Tassell throughout the years of his life, was a gift that was far more valuable than any material possession. Grandma Tassell faithfully prayed for her two grandsons, Albert and Paul. After Paul finished reading Ephesians every morning, Grandma prayed that the two boys would hear the call of God and become preachers of the gospel of Jesus Christ. Paul has often said, "I am in the ministry today as an answer to Grandma's prayers."

In the last year of Grandma's life, Pastor Jeremiah often came to the house to visit her. He always read a Scripture

passage and prayed for Grandma. During those visits he
turned to young Paul and asked, "Paul, can you spell
Deuteronomy?" Paul's answer was a timid "No, sir." Then
Pastor Jeremiah challenged the young boy with a reward of
a shiny new nickel if he could spell the book of the Bible
correctly by his next visit. For the lure of a nickel, Paul
Tassell always met the challenge.

The Gospel Tabernacle was the largest evangelical
church in Toledo. For twenty-nine years Dr. Louis Ziemer
was the pastor, and the Tassell family occasionally went to
the Gospel Tabernacle to hear him preach. Dr. Ziemer also
found time in his busy schedule to visit and pray with
Grandma on her sickbed. Before Dr. Ziemer would pray, he
put anointing oil on Grandma's forehead. At nine years of
age, Paul found himself fascinated by this practice, yet he
never mustered the courage to ask the revered preacher
why he did it.

On the night of August 16, 1944, Albert and Paul
Tassell sat just outside their grandmother's bedroom listening as her breathing grew weaker and weaker. That night
her breathing stopped and she died, but what she had
prayed into the hearts of those two boys would go on living
and affecting lives for Christ for the rest of the century.

STANDING TALL

So here were three common women who never made
the national news and who never received their "fifteen
minutes of fame." Yet they made up a terrific trio: a mother,
sensitive to her son's tears and searching heart; an aunt,
patient with a boy's childish persistence and wise to use it
for his gain; and a grandmother, believing in the power of
prayer to produce a faithful man of God. Insignificant? Yes,

by the world's standard these three were not educated, wealthy, or famous. However, by Heaven's standard this terrific trio stands tall, having been used of God to fan the flames of a gospel preacher in the heart of a boy. That same boy would become a man pounding on the pulpits of America, preaching the life-changing Word of God with passion, persistence, and powerful prayer.

NOTES

Opening Page: Ihre Freundin, quoted by Lloyd Cory, compiler, *Quotable Quotations* (Wheaton, Ill.: Victor Books, 1985), 432.

1. William Ross Wallace, quoted by John Bartlett, compiler, *Familiar Quotations* (Garden City, N.J.: Garden City Publishing Co., 1944), 534.

Lightweight Champion of the World

Follow me, and I will make you fishers of men.

MATTHEW 4:19

SPORTS has invaded—and may be the one thing that has conquered—American culture. Great athletes from the "Great Bambino" Babe Ruth to Muhammad Ali to Mark "Big Mac" McGwire to Tiger Woods have become our heroes. It really doesn't matter if their personal lifestyles are pagan and debauched or clean and righteous. If they can perform in the arena, produce revenue for the owner, and party all night with adoring fans, they can be king. Their faithful followers will bow to their wishes and overlook their character faults. Nothing else matters if our team wins the Super Bowl!

Multimillion-dollar contracts seem to be signed daily. Product endorsements make nineteen-year-olds wealthy beyond imagination. The kids of American society turn these muscle-bound intellectual midgets into their heroes because of their bulging bank accounts and bawdy

29

lifestyles. Where did all of this begin? The answer is in Genesis. Nimrod became the first human that the kids would want to imitate. There really is nothing new under the sun. In 1944, Paul Tassell's hero was a welterweight prizefighter named Vince Foster.

MR. TOUGH GUY

Al and Paul's father was a semiprofessional boxer. When the boys were ten and eleven, their dad gave them both a set of boxing gloves, and he taught his sons how to use them. Al was much more peace-loving than Paul. Even with much coaxing, he could not be persuaded to duke it out with his younger brother. As a result, Paul had to find other neighborhood guys on which to vent his wrath. At thirteen, Paul had one ambition: to become the lightweight champion of the world by the time he reached age twenty.

Sports had become very big in the mind of this teenager. Boxing and softball took up all of his spare time. Paul played shortstop on the junior high softball team. Their team was good, and they won the county championship. However, even with Paul's mind and body taken up with the pursuit of athletics, the Holy Spirit was beginning to work on Paul's heart. God began dealing with this young teen about forsaking his own plans so he would know the will of God for his life and do it with all of his strength.

A FERVENT PRAYER AND A KNOCKOUT PUNCH

In those early teen years, two events took place in Paul Tassell's life that God used to formulate his thinking and direct his steps. The first took place in the Toledo

Gospel Tabernacle on a Sunday night. As Dr. Ziemer was preaching, the Holy Spirit began to squeeze the heart of two teenagers. There was no audible voice, but it was as if the Spirit of God were whispering in their ears, "Your Heavenly Father is calling you." Ziemer's message came to a close, the invitation hymn was being sung, and the brothers had come to decision time. Not exactly sure what was going to happen, they stepped from their pew into the aisle and slowly walked to the front. At that point something unusual took place. Dr. Ziemer stepped from his place and left the platform. He put his arms around Al and Paul and prayed fervently that Almighty God in the power of His Son's name would make great preachers of the boys. The impact of that moment and the fervency of that prayer stayed with Paul Tassell for the rest of his life.

The second event took place in July 1948. Paul's youth pastor, Douglas Beason, talked Paul into going to the Regular Baptist Camp at Lake O'Dell, Ohio. In the middle of that week, the camp evangelist, missionary pastor Ed Morrell, illustrated one of his messages with some comments on the life of Paul's hero, welterweight prizefighter Vince Foster. Foster was being touted to fight Sugar Ray Robinson for the championship. Foster talked about being a Christian and often boasted that he always carried a New Testament. When the Spirit was wooing Paul to Christian service, Paul tried to suppress Him by pointing to Foster and arguing, "See, a man can be a great athlete and have a lot of influence for Christ." Yet he knew in his heart of hearts that he was making an idol out of a mere mortal. On July 20, 1948 (Paul's fourteenth birthday), in the middle of his sermon, Ed Morrell held up a newspaper article announcing that on the previous night, Vince Foster had been killed in an automobile accident in which he was drunk and in the arms of another man's wife.

That was the Holy Spirit's knockout punch. It was a blow that hit Paul squarely in the heart and buckled his knees. No longer would there be any rationalization. There would be no more arguing with God. Jesus was the true champion, and Paul would be in His corner. On that night Paul Norman Tassell knew exactly what God wanted him to be—a preacher of the gospel of Jesus Christ. He made his decision that night and never looked back.

That same week a camp counselor gave Paul a book authored by Robert Cook titled *Now That I Believe*. It had a profound impact on his life. Cook stressed the importance of the Word of God in the life of the believer. At fourteen, Paul determined to read the Bible an hour every day. His only problem was finding a quiet place in his house with three sisters. However, he found that quiet place between the kitchen and the basement on the downstairs landing. Paul spent his time with the Lord from four to five o'clock. Those sessions changed his life.

A ROOKIE PREACHER

One year later, in September 1949, Paul Tassell preached his first sermon—at a youth rally sponsored by a Christian bookstore. Beulah Lewis operated that store in Sylvania, Ohio, and invited the young preacher to give the message. Beulah saw the potential in the budding preacher and to this day still prays for Paul Tassell. It was also that same year that Paul saw a full-page advertisement for Bob Jones University in the *Christian Herald* magazine. The ad stated that an academy was available for high school students. He decided Bob Jones was the place to prepare for ministry.

A YOUNG MAN'S DECISION

Becoming champion of the world or hearing and heeding God's call? It is a question young men must answer almost every day. The enticements of the world are strong, and the world's voices of fame and prosperity are loud. If the flesh allows them to, they can drown out the call of God in the ears of young men. On the other hand, when a young man is consistently prayed for, is influenced by godly leaders, and is encouraged to go to godly places such as Sunday School and Christian camp, he is a wise individual who will not allow the clamoring world to drown out the voice of God. That young man may never experience the world's wealth, but it is not important to him. He may receive some notoriety, but for the most part he will probably not be well known because he will spend his entire life pointing people to Someone greater than himself. It is obviously not a life for everyone, yet there are a few chosen men who will expend their lives for God's call of duty. Paul Norman Tassell was one of God's chosen. Paul made the best choice of his life, to heed God's call.

CHAPTER THREE

Bob Jones University

*Let every student be plainly instructed and earnestly pressed
to . . . lay Christ in the bottom as the only foundation
of all knowledge and learning.*

JOHN HARVARD

THE day before Paul's fifteenth birthday, one more son joined the Tassell family. They named the baby Jerry. Just a few months later, on January 22, 1950, Paul's father, his mother holding the baby, brother Al, and Paul's three sisters stood at the front door of the Tassell home as his father led in prayer. After the prayer they were going to load the car and head for Bob Jones University and Academy. Paul was the first one to leave home, and this event turned out to be much more emotional than anyone had planned. As Albert prayed, he suddenly began to cry. Young Paul was shocked because he had never seen that big man cry before. His mother began to weep softly, and then all three sisters began to bawl. Tassell's older brother, Al, did not cry because he was finally going to get the bedroom to himself. As Paul stood in the family circle, he prayed silently, "Lord, I don't care who

cries or for how long; I believe you have called me seven
hundred miles away to hone my skills as a preacher, and
no earthly tie can be strong enough to pull me away from
the will of God." Finally, after what seemed like a millen-
nium, his father regained his composure and finished the
prayer. There were final hugs, then Paul, Al, and their father got into their 1948 Pontiac and headed for Bob Jones
in Greenville, South Carolina.

On His Way!

Since Paul Tassell had never been more than fifty
miles away from home, this trip was quite an adventure.
The men drove straight through, with Al sharing some of
the driving time. At age fifteen, Paul was too young to
have a license. He did not realize that his first trip of traveling mountain roads with hairpin curves and speed limits
of up to thirty-five miles an hour would eventually lead
him to travel hundreds of thousands of miles across
America. He would crisscross the land by plane, train, and
automobile, preaching in almost every state of the Union.

For any fifteen-year-old, driving onto the Bob Jones
campus can be a daunting, intimidating experience. Its
rich and unusual history, large cream-colored buildings,
famous faculty, and strict discipline can cause even those
youth with the stoutest of hearts to cringe a little. On the
other hand, knowing God wants one there to study and
prepare for ministry diminishes the fear and replaces it
with the excitement of anticipation.

Chapel Services

The chapel service was the focal point of each day of
school. Tassell's assigned chapel seat was on the second

row in the Rodeheaver Auditorium. On that platform, some of the greatest, best-known preachers in the world expounded the Scriptures, preaching to eager young college students and motivating them to give their lives to win the hearts of mankind for Jesus Christ.

One of the first chapel services that Tassell attended had the student body buzzing. World-renowned evangelist Billy Graham was the speaker. To Paul he seemed like a veritable giant as he stood just a few feet away preaching the gospel. Graham had just finished crusades in Los Angeles and Boston and was on his way to Columbia, South Carolina, when he stopped at Bob Jones. Of course, those were the days before Graham's compromising with liberals. Graham could fan the flames of passion for Christ in the hearts of the "preacher boys." Sitting in that auditorium with three thousand people listening to Graham and other great preachers was indeed an awesome and heart-stirring experience for a fifteen-year-old boy.

JUMPING AHEAD

In the spring of 1951, Tassell completed his junior year of high school at the academy. Back home in Toledo that summer, he took correspondence courses to complete the required number of credits to skip his senior year of high school. Arriving back on the BJU campus in the fall of 1951, Tassell went into a room where some military veterans were taking college entrance exams. Paul blended in with the rest of the college hopefuls and took the exams. A day or two later, Dr. Theodore Mercer, the registrar, called Tassell into his office and asked what he was doing by taking those exams. Paul explained about taking the summer correspondence courses and his de-

sire to skip his senior year of high school and enroll as a
college freshman. Mercer told Tassell that he had very
high scores on the test; and after sizing up that skinny kid
from Toledo, he decided that if Paul could maintain a C
average, he would allow him to enroll and remain at the
college level. Paul Norman Tassell had become a college
student.

A SOLID WORK ETHIC

The cost of attending Bob Jones University in 1951
was $700 a year for room, board, and tuition. That ex-
pense meant that Tassell had to raise $70 per month to
pay his college bills. In those days he was athletically
"lean and mean." He bought an old Schwinn bicycle for
$5 from a New Jersey student named George Morgan
and took a morning paper route delivering the *Greenville
News*. Paul was no stranger to the work ethic. He had
been a paperboy in Toledo, beginning at age thirteen.
However, his Greenville route was much more demand-
ing. His alarm went off at 3:45 every morning. At that
time, BJU was considered out in the country, and
Tassell's route was on the other side of the city. By the
time he peddled across town, folded his papers, delivered
them, and rode back to campus, it was seven o'clock. His
first class was at eight.

Tassell made enough money to get through the year
because of the larger route he had on Sunday. Carrying
the big bag across his shoulders, he rode his old bike and
hurled those papers at the front doors of his customers.
Paul was introduced to one large challenge during his
first round of collecting. One of his customers owned a
large, vicious, red chowhound. The man told Tassell, "If

he gives you a hard time, kill him, cuz he's the biggest, meanest thing around here." The paperboy quickly secured a two-foot-long iron pipe for his own protection. Every morning for a year he took two or three healthy swings at that red chow but never connected. Through the years, as he visited in countless homes and all kinds of neighborhoods, Paul Tassell always maintained an intelligent respect for dogs, large or small.

The loss of so much healthy sleep was not a wise thing for that young college student. At the end of his freshman year, therefore, he gave up the paper route and took a weekend job at Kash-n-Karry. He worked on Friday nights from seven to nine o'clock and on Saturdays from seven in the morning to nine at night. His main job was cutting up chickens. During his sophomore year he got a job on the BJU dining room cleanup crew. His crew chief was Donald Camp, who later pastored Grace Baptist Church in Anderson, Indiana, for twenty-two years. Ironically, both Camp and Tassell were diagnosed with Parkinson's disease later in life.

AN INTERRUPTION

Paul's father, Albert, suffered with chronic bronchitis. At the end of Paul's sophomore year, his dad was critically ill and could not work to support the family. Paul returned home, and in the fall of 1953, he and his brother, Al, both enrolled at the University of Toledo. It was there Paul completed his junior year, while he and Al worked four-to-midnight jobs to support the family. Their father recovered from the severe sickness, and Al went on to Detroit Bible College. Paul returned to Bob Jones University for his senior year.

EXTRACURRICULAR ACTIVITIES

Every student at Bob Jones joins a society. Tassell
aligned himself with the NIKONIAN Literary Society. He
played soccer and volleyball for the NIKONIAN Conquerors. His first soccer game turned out to be a disaster. While
racing after the ball, his opponent's cleated foot took off the
top half of his sneaker and the big toenail of his right foot.
He walked on crutches for a week after that game. The volleyball team fared much better. Tassell at the grand height
of five feet seven inches set the ball for the big boys to do
the spiking. The combination worked, and the Conquerors
had a championship team. But athletics had to take a
backseat to much more important matters that arrived with
the onset of Tassell's senior year at BJU.

At the beginning of each school year, hundreds of
"preacher boys," under the guidance of Dr. Gilbert
Stenholm, chose places of Christian service. There were
jail ministries, street meetings, Saturday-night youth rallies, door-to-door visitation; a few were able to get preaching assignments at churches for the Sunday morning and
evening services.

In September 1954, Paul Tassell joined a team ministry
with Waldo Yeager and Martin Kraft. The three Bible students decided to hold children's meetings in the neighborhoods of Elberton, Georgia. Elberton was a town of seven
thousand people located eighty miles from the BJU campus. The young men spent Saturday mornings going door-
to-door inviting boys and girls to the afternoon session.
They used the latest flannelgraph and always gave a clear
presentation of the gospel of Jesus Christ. Many young
people professed Christ as Savior.

On the first Sunday morning they were in Elberton, the

three young preachers decided to go to the poorer section of town to three different churches. Tassell attended Second Baptist Church, Yeager went to Gordon Street Methodist Church, and Kraft headed to Northside Baptist Church. All three of these churches had white frame buildings with no central air-conditioning or heating (unless you call a pot-bellied stove central heating)! They planned to introduce themselves to the pastors and ask if they could be used in teaching Sunday School. They also wanted to advertise their Saturday-afternoon children's Bible class.

MR. TASSELL BECOMES PASTOR TASSELL

It was the second Sunday of September 1954 when Paul Tassell walked into Second Baptist Church of Elberton, Georgia, and asked to see the pastor. A deacon met him at the front door and explained to him that they had no pastor. Paul then asked to see the adult-class Sunday School teacher. The deacon said that the teacher would not be there that morning. Paul then asked if they had a substitute teacher for the adult class and was told no. Without hesitating, Tassell told the deacon he would be willing to teach the class, and the man seemed genuinely delighted. The deacon introduced Paul to the folks as "the preacher from Bob Jones." After the class, the people started preparing to go home, since there was no pastor. But Tassell said, "Don't go home; just let me preach." So they stayed for a worship service, and Tassell preached the Word of God. When the service was over, the deacon invited Paul back to preach the message that evening, and he happily agreed.

Waldo, Martin, and Paul were staying in a $5-a-night hotel room. They had agreed to meet there after the morning services to pool their meager resources for lunch. Instead, when they met at the hotel, they found that all three had received invitations for southern fried chicken from the generous, hospitable people of Elberton.

That evening Waldo and Martin attended the churches where they would be teaching Sunday School. Paul went back and preached at Second Baptist Church. After the message he turned the pulpit over to a deacon named Edgar Hanvey, who immediately called the church into a business session and said, "The deacons would like to recommend Paul Tassell to be our pastor." Someone made the motion, and there was a second. Someone else called for a ballot vote. In less than five minutes (talk about a surprise), the deacons announced the vote: sixteen "yes" votes and zero "no" votes. It was a unanimous call. Tassell took the pulpit and accepted on the spot. The deacons told him the salary would be $17.50 a week. In addition, they would take a love offering on the last Sunday of the month to help with expenses.

Paul Tassell thus became Pastor Tassell. There would be no more bicycle rides around Greenville. No more cutting up chickens in Kash-n-Karry. No more sweeping up the BJU dining room floors. Paul was twenty years old, a senior at a renowned Christian university, and pastor of a beloved flock at Second Baptist Church of Elberton, Georgia. From the second Sunday of September 1954 to the last Sunday of August 1958, Paul Tassell had the privilege of pastoring that church.

NOTES

Opening Page: John Harvard, quoted by Roy B. Zuck, compiler, *The Speaker's Quote Book* (Grand Rapids: Kregel Publications, 1997), 126.

Second Baptist Church, Elberton, Georgia

*A preacher who is too big for a little crowd
would be too little for a big crowd.*

VANCE HAVNER

AN old man, walking on the beach at dawn, . . . noticed a young man ahead of him picking up starfish and flinging them into the sea. Catching up with the youth, he asked him what he was doing. The answer was that the stranded starfish would die if left until the morning sun.

" 'But the beach goes on for miles, and there are millions of starfish,' countered the old man. 'How can your effort make any difference?'

"The young man looked at the starfish in his hand and then threw it to safety in the waves. 'It makes a difference to this one,' he replied."[1]

Whatever happened to the word "lost"? Do we as Christians really believe mankind is lost without Christ and bound for Hell? Do we believe we have *any* responsibility to point men and women to Christ? Our churches

seem to be more like trading posts instead of headquar-
ters for sending search and rescue teams out for lost humanity. We trade Christians back and forth like trading
baseball cards, depending on the style of worship or
which preacher is hot at the time. It's time we got back
that evangelistic zeal, growing our churches with new
converts and teaching them to reach others with the good
news of salvation through Christ.

THE EVANGELIST

Paul Tassell was an evangelist from his first days of
ministry. Coming out of the local eatery on his first official
Sunday as pastor of Second Baptist Church, he looked
across the street and noticed a man sitting in his car
parked by the curb. Tassell walked up to the young man,
introduced himself, and offered him a gospel tract. As he
began explaining the gospel story, the young man's eyes
filled with tears. He looked up at Tassell and said, "This is
what I have been looking for." His name was Joe Wallace.
He was twenty years old; and, like thousands of others in
Elberton, he carved out a living in a granite quarry.

At that moment the young preacher urged the young
man to believe on the Lord Jesus Christ. Joe Wallace
prayed the prayer of a sinner and became a child of God.
When Joe finished praying, Paul prayed, thanking God for
saving Joe and asking God to help Joe grow in his
newfound faith. When Paul finished praying, Joe looked up
and said his wife needed to hear about Christ. Paul got into
Joe's car, and the two of them went to pick up Winnie at the
telephone office. As they were driving to their apartment,
Joe told Winnie what he had done. Paul sat by as Joe, this
brand-new believer, lovingly led his wife to Christ.

Joe Wallace had two older brothers with families, and he also led them to Christ over a period of a few months. On a Sunday night, Tassell baptized three Wallace families and they became members of Second Baptist Church. Joe Wallace later became a Sunday School teacher and a deacon at Second Baptist. In 1998, Joe Wallace went to Heaven, a victim of lung cancer brought on by forty years of working in the quarries.

SECOND IN EVERYTHING

The building that housed Second Baptist Church was an old-fashioned white frame structure built on blocks at the four corners. The congregation decided to close in the crawl space with carefully chiseled granite, so six men, including their pastor, met at the church at seven o'clock on a hot Saturday morning in July and got busy. About nine-thirty deacon Ed Hanvey came to where Paul was working and said, "Pastor, this is not Toledo, Ohio; this is Elberton, Georgia. You are working too fast and too hard to last in this climate." Being the self-confident young man he was, Tassell ignored Hanvey's advice and an hour later collapsed with heatstroke. The experience greatly added to his humility and to the sympathy with which his southern brethren looked upon their Yankee pastor.

Second Baptist Church was located on a dirt road and, in appearing to live up to its name, it seemed to come in second in just about every aspect. It was located across the tracks from the big, beautiful First Baptist Church pastored by Dr. Herman Ihley. In Second's middle aisle stood a potbellied stove, the only means to heat the building in the winter. In the cold months those who sat in the front roasted, and those in the back froze. In the dog days of summer everyone was hot. There was no indoor plumbing. In fact, there was no outdoor plumbing either.

One day in the mail, Pastor Tassell received a note from Dr. Ihley that read, "I talked to the deacons last night concerning the good work you are doing at Second Baptist. We, upon your approval, would like to have installed in your building propane gas heaters in each corner." Tassell responded, "We gladly accept your generosity." Dr. Ihley also knew of Tassell's need for a dependable automobile. He sold Paul his 1941 Pontiac for $50. The terms of the agreement were $5 down and $5 a month until it was paid off.

AN OFFER AND A REFUSAL

About a year or so later, Tassell received another note from Dr. Ihley, this time requesting a Saturday morning meeting in Dr. Ihley's office. Paul noted that Ihley was a winsome, wily, and witty man who enjoyed preaching to his congregation of five hundred and holding revival services two or three times a year out in the more rural areas of Georgia. Dr. Ihley asked Paul to sit down and got right to the point. He said he had met earlier in the week with his deacons and they had come to an agreement that First Baptist Church would send Paul to Louisville Seminary and pay all of his expenses for their three-year Master of Divinity course. Dr. Ihley also said that at the end of the three years he would see to it that Paul got a large Southern Baptist pastorate in the state of Georgia.

At that point in the meeting, Paul asked Dr. Ihley the obvious question: "What's the catch?" Ihley responded, "Give up the kind of ecclesiastical separation preached by Bob Jones and the rest of the BJU faculty." Without hesitation Tassell replied that was too great a price to pay and that he could not accept his offer. What hair Dr. Ihley had left was red, and when he stood up behind his desk, that hair stood up with him. He announced, "Paul, you are making a big mistake." Tassell responded, "I cannot sacrifice my convictions." With that statement the meeting ended abruptly and uncomfortably. Dr. Ihley was later made state secretary for the North Carolina Baptist Convention. He has since gone Home to be with the Lord.

ON THE AIR

In addition to finishing his schooling, preparing two sermons a week, and visiting the hospital on Sunday afternoons, Paul also began doing a live radio broadcast on Sunday afternoons. He broadcast the gospel of Jesus Christ from one of the local stations serving the seven thousand people of Elberton. This was his first attempt at radio ministry, and the experience would serve him well in the years to come.

PASTOR TASSELL BECOMES DR. TASSELL

Paul continued his education at Bob Jones while he was pastoring in Elberton. He went to school year-round with no time off from September 1954 to May 1958. He majored in New Testament interpretation and minored in church history. On May 28, 1958, Tassell, at the age of twenty-three, graduated with a doctor of philosophy in New Testament interpretation.

FOND MEMORIES

Tassell has many fond memories of Second Baptist Church in Elberton, Georgia. That is where he cut his teeth in ministry. That is where he learned that Sundays come every week, and either you are prepared or you are not. That is where he learned that ministry is serving the Lord by serving people. That is where he learned that one grows a church by evangelizing the lost, feeding the flock on the solid food of God's Word, and staying on your knees in prayer while believing God can do the impossible. Elberton was a good training and proving ground for this young preacher. Tassell passed the test and was ready for God to direct his steps for further service.

NOTES

Opening Page: Vance Havner, quoted by Dennis J. Hester, compiler, *The Vance Havner Quote Book* (Grand Rapids: Baker Book House, 1986), 169.

1. Hugh Duncan, quoted by Zuck, 134.

Doris Jaeger

*Whoso findeth a wife findeth a good thing,
and obtaineth favour of the LORD.*

PROVERBS 18:22

ON October the seventh in the year of our Lord nineteen hundred fifty-four, Paul Norman Tassell's life would change forever. Listen to what happened in his words: "It was an enchanted evening when I looked across the BJU dining room and saw a blue-eyed, red-headed young woman who made me completely forget the seven other people sitting at my table. They thought something was terribly wrong with me, because I had become paralyzed and completely unable to pass the food." Paul finally recovered his voice and asked one of the girls sitting at his table if she knew the redhead sitting several tables away. Paul asked her if she would do him a great favor by getting the redhead's name and bringing it to him the next morning at breakfast. He told her, "If you will do this for me, I will be forever grateful."

The next morning Paul's informant, Fran, brought the information he had requested. The redhead's name was Doris Jaeger. She was a junior majoring in elementary education. Paul said to Fran, "I will be forever grateful to you." Immediately after breakfast, Paul headed straight for Doris. Suddenly he was standing before her with his heart beating so fast and so loud he was sure everyone in the room must be able to hear it. His first words to Doris were, "Hi, I'm Paul Tassell."

She said, "So."

"So I'd like to carry your books and walk you to class."

She said, "That would be nice." Those were the lightest heavy books he had ever carried.

DORIS'S HOME LIFE

May Doris Jaeger grew up in a Plymouth Brethren family on a poultry farm just outside Trenton, New Jersey, near Princeton University. She was born at home and lived her entire life in the same house before going to Bob Jones. Doris was the second of three children. Her older sister, Isobel (named after their mother), also went to Bob Jones. Doris's younger brother, Donald, became a cabinetmaker and finish carpenter par excellence.

During World War II, Mr. Jaeger worked in a factory making airplanes for the war effort, and he also learned the skill of making mattresses. After the war he combined the mattress making with poultry farming. Mrs. Jaeger, affectionately known as Nana, was born in 1900 into a large family of eleven children. Times were hard in Scotland, so in 1923, her family moved to Kapuskasing, Ontario, Canada. After enduring one winter, they moved

south, first to Niagara Falls and then to New Jersey.
There Isobel met Asher Jaeger in a Plymouth Brethren
meeting. In 1929, Asher, whom everyone called "Happy,"
and Isobel were married. Happy and Isobel set a tremendous example for their children. They taught them how to
work hard and have a happy home.

Doris grew up and finished high school. Then it was
time for college. She left for Bob Jones in 1951, complet-
ing her freshman and sophomore years in '52 and '53. She
went home to work a year in '53 but returned to the BJU
campus in the fall of '54 to start her junior year. Then Paul
Tassell walked into her life.

NEWLYWEDS

On August 4, 1956, at the Woodside Gospel Chapel in
Trenton, New Jersey, Paul and Doris became husband
and wife. A Plymouth Brethren preacher named William
Bryson performed the ceremony. Paul and Doris went on
a weeklong honeymoon in the Pocono Mountains of
Pennsylvania. There they rented a cabin for five days for
just $15.

When that week concluded, they headed back to
Greenville so Paul could continue pastoring at Second
Baptist Church and working on his Ph.D. Doris immediately secured a teaching position in the Greenville public
school system. She was given a most challenging class in
one of the roughest mill districts of Greenville. It was a
fourth-grade class with thirty-six students, thirty-one of
whom were boys. The principal gave Doris a paddle and a
Bible and told her to use both as she wished. Doris used
that Bible hundreds of times during the year and led most
of those ornery kids to Christ. Back then no one minded

if the teacher started the day by reading the Scriptures and leading the class in prayer.

Paul and Doris purchased a twenty-nine-foot mobile home with an extra room built on the back. They bought it for $750 from Gene Gurganus, who became a pioneer missionary to Bangladesh. Besides being a great preacher, Gene also became a great linguist and superb recruiter of missionary candidates for the Association of Baptists for World Evangelism. The lot rent for the mobile home, which included water and electricity, was $13 a month. Paul and Doris sold the mobile home two years later to an up-and-coming graduate student for $750. Paul and Doris figured that $13 a month rent for two years was not bad at all!

CONTINUED MINISTRY IN ELBERTON

On Friday afternoons when Doris got home from school, the young couple loaded the car and headed for Elberton. They usually arrived in time for supper with a church member. Most of the time they ate with Edgar and Jo Hanvey and their five children. On Friday evenings both Doris and Paul did some hospital visitation, and Paul prepared for his radio broadcast on Sunday afternoons. Saturdays found the couple teaching child evangelism classes in the poorer neighborhoods. Paul spent Saturday evenings working on his Sunday sermons. After the Sunday evening service, they left for home and arrived sometime before midnight. Paul's first class was at eight o'clock on Monday mornings. He remembers many wonderful naps during that Hebrew class. The Tassells kept up this schedule from September 1956 through May 1958, when Paul graduated and they moved to Elberton.

Throughout the summer of 1958, something was stirring in the heart of Paul Tassell. Was the Lord preparing
him to leave? For almost three months he pushed those
feelings and thoughts aside. Then on a Saturday night late
in August 1958, Paul was sitting on a brand-new couch he
and Doris had just purchased from George Johnson, who
owned the furniture store in town. He said to Doris, "I'm
resigning in the morning." Earlier that week Joe Bower,
who was then pastoring Emmanuel Baptist Church in Toledo, had called Paul and encouraged him to come home.
"You should be ordained in your home church. I will help
you find a church to pastor," he had told Paul.

The next morning after the service, Paul read his letter
of resignation to the people of Second Baptist Church. That
Sunday night was one of the most difficult of the Tassells'
lives. Paul and Doris cried so hard that their ribs hurt for
four days. Mr. Johnson at the furniture store agreed to take
back all the things the Tassells had bought and used for
only three months. Paul and Doris packed all their belongings into their Chevy and headed north to Toledo.

Bethany Baptist Church, Galesburg, Illinois

The Christian church is the only society in the world in which membership is based upon the qualification that the candidate shall be unworthy of membership.

CHARLES C. MORRISON

CHARLES Haddon Spurgeon and D. L. Moody were never ordained. Both men were uniquely gifted servants of God. Spurgeon believed that because he was a minister, he should never receive authority and commission from men. He also believed in what he called the glorious principle of independence; that is, every church having the right to call its own ministers, and who cares if they are ordained or not or if the whole world likes or dislikes the choice. His last objection to ordination was that he could find no real meaning in its ceremony. Spurgeon asked, "Where is the scriptural warrant for such nonsense?" He went on to say that "most ordinations were merely 'placing empty hands on empty heads.' "[1]

Though Spurgeon and Moody might disagree with the practice, Baptist ministers of the gospel have been ordained by churches through the centuries. If the practice of ordination has value, it is because it is a valid way of publicly acknowledging what God has already done in the heart of a man. If ordination is done with the call of God and the souls of mankind in mind, then accountability becomes a major factor. The ordination council, if rigorously used, can help a church determine whether or not a man is qualified for ministry.

A THREE-HOUR EXAMINATION

Paul Tassell was probably better prepared for ordination than most men, in that he had just completed his oral exams for his Ph.D. All he took to the lectern that day was his Bible. With his knowledge and enthusiasm for the Word of God, "Dr. Paul" actually enjoyed the three-hour examination. Lynn Rogers served as the moderator for the ordination council. James T. Jeremiah preached the ordination sermon. Pastor Joseph Bower suggested that the church take an offering for Paul to buy books for his personal library. Down through the years, many books have become close personal friends to Dr. Paul, as God gave him a love for reading and studying. His preaching called upon many sources as he dug for just the right word or just the right illustration, mining from the many books, periodicals, and magazines with which he surrounded himself.

THE WORK GOD BEGAN
IN GALESBURG

Ordination usually has some side benefits for the candidates. One of those benefits is that the candidate is introduced to pastors and laymen who in turn can be used of God to open doors of ministry opportunity. After the ordination service, the Tassell family returned home to the ringing of the telephone. On the other end was a man named Paul Montgomery, a childhood friend and a fellow Bob Jones graduate. Montgomery was the principal of a large Christian academy in Peoria, Illinois. He had a fascinating story to tell about a citywide evangelistic campaign conducted by evangelist Merv Rosell in the fall of 1956. Sixty people from East Main Street Congregational Church of Galesburg, Illinois, believed in Jesus Christ as Savior. They went back to their church on Sunday morning, and after the service they crowded into a Sunday School room with the same question on each of their lips. "Why doesn't our pastor preach the gospel like Merv Rosell?" They demanded some answers and then concluded that their pastor was a Bible-denying liberal. Those sixty people made some courageous decisions. First, they would call for their pastor's resignation. They determined to start a new church if they failed in their attempt to rid themselves of the false teacher. The vote to oust the pastor did not carry. They lost by one vote. Their emotions swirling, they left some family and friends and started a new church. They called this new work Bethany Conservative Congregational Church.

God is always on time. Just as that new church was forming, Swedish Covenant Church in Galesburg decided to sell its Bethany Chapel property. Those sixty people stepped out on faith and unanimously decided to buy the property for the fledgling church. The auditorium had seating for ninety people, and there were four Sunday School rooms in the basement. The original pastor's study was one of the four Sunday School rooms.

"YOU ARE THE MAN"

Paul Montgomery had heard about this new church from one of his thirteen-year-old students, named John W. Carlson. Montgomery took it upon himself to aid the new church in getting pulpit supply, or good speakers, in the following months. With a growing fervency in his voice that could not be lessened by the poor telephone connection between Peoria and Toledo, Montgomery told Paul Tassell, "I believe with all my heart, you are the man for this church." He continued by explaining how he had introduced the young congregation to the *Sword of the Lord* newspaper and *The Baptist Bulletin* magazine. The new church was taking tremendous strides in positioning itself as a Baptist congregation. Montgomery urged Tassell to say yes to a speaking engagement on Sunday, November 9, 1958, for both the morning and evening services. He suggested that Paul and Doris drive to Peoria and spend Friday and Saturday with him and his wife, and then on Sunday morning they would make the one-hour drive to Galesburg, a city of approximately forty thousand.

The drive to Galesburg that Sunday morning was uneventful. The conversation in the car was minimal, light at best. However, something unique was about to happen. God was about to call a specific man to a specific place to do a specific work. It was not tension in the air; it was excitement.

When Dr. Paul walked into that ninety-seat auditorium, he was overwhelmed to find that the congregation of sixty had swelled to ninety-seven. Years later Dr. Paul would describe that morning with these words: "What singing! What praying! What enthusiasm!" It truly was love at first sight. Tassell spent the afternoon with the officers of the church, explaining to them who he was, what he believed, and that if they called him to be their pastor, he would lead them to change their name to Bethany Baptist Church and to affiliate with the General Association of Regular Baptist Churches (GARBC). The church asked Tassell to stay until Wednesday night, when they would vote on him.

THE VOTE IS IN

The excitement meter was registering in the red when Paul and Doris returned to Peoria. Dr. Paul immediately called Dr. Jeremiah, who had made arrangements for him to speak at Grace Baptist Church in Cedarville, Ohio, on November 23. Tassell told Jeremiah with confidence that he would receive the necessary votes on Wednesday night to become the pastor of Bethany. He also asked Jeremiah as graciously as he could to release him from the Cedarville obligation. Dr. Jeremiah did so with a cautious warning: "There has been many a slip between Sunday night and Wednesday night."

However, on Wednesday night the vote was thirty-eight "yes" votes and zero "no" votes to call Paul Tassell as pastor. The Tassells returned to Toledo and stayed until Thanksgiving Day. It was the last time the entire Tassell family would be gathered together in one place. After dinner it began to snow. Paul and Doris decided to leave for Galesburg early in the morning. It snowed hard all night, and the roads were treacherous. However, early in the morning, with all their earthly possessions loaded into their 1953 Chevrolet, Paul and Doris headed for Galesburg, Illinois.

A SLIDE, A SCARE, AND A SEDAN

About a hundred miles out of Toledo, tragedy struck.

The right rear tire went off the side of the pavement and turned the car sideways. The car slid out of control while going about thirty-five miles per hour and headed straight for a 1950 Ford sedan. The lady in the Ford braked, but on the snow-covered roads the brakes were more of a hazard than a help. There were two suitcases between Doris and the passenger-side door, which God used to save her life as the Ford slammed into the front door on the passenger side. A trucker traveling behind the Tassell vehicle managed to miss hitting either car and bring his rig to a stop. As the trucker ran to help, Paul yelled that he and Doris were all right and that he should check on the occupants of the Ford instead. At the same time a state trooper and an ambulance arrived on the scene. The driver of the Ford was a young woman in her thirties. She had broken some ribs on the steering wheel. Her sixteen-year-old daughter had smashed through the windshield, sustaining injuries requiring a trip to the hospital. Both mother and daughter fully recovered from the accident.

After the ambulance took the woman and her daughter away, the trucker, state trooper, and firefighters turned their attention to the Tassell car. They had to use a crowbar to get Paul and Doris out of the wrecked vehicle. The car's trunk had popped open on impact. Dr. Paul recalls how his heart sank when he looked down the road to see all of his books, clothes, and other possessions scattered over two hundred yards down the snowy highway. Paul and Doris thanked God they were still alive. Later they realized that their hair and clothes were covered in shattered glass, but there were no bleeding wounds. Paul remembers thinking to himself, "The Devil must really not want us to go to Galesburg."

The state trooper took Paul and Doris to the house of the pastor of a small Baptist church in the next town. There they were able to calm down, call Paul's dad back in Toledo, and inform their insurance agent about the accident. The insurance man sold the car for parts, and the money was enough for train tickets to Galesburg. Mr. Tassell and Paul's brother, Al, came the next day with a large Buick sedan and piled what was left of the young couple's belongings into the trunk and delivered them to Galesburg.

Upon arriving in Galesburg, the Tassells were greeted by Mrs. Albert Muffley. She told them that Bob Swanson wanted to speak with them down at his Texaco station. Paul and Doris borrowed a car and drove to Swanson's station. There Bob handed them the keys to a shiny black 1950 Buick Super four-door sedan with Dynaflow drive. The church had collected the money and bought that car for the Tassells. What a surprising welcome to Galesburg for the new young pastor and his wife!

A NEW HOME

It had been arranged for the Tassells to stay with the Muffleys until the parsonage was ready. Albert and his wife were in their youthful eighties, and both expected to live to a hundred. Mr. Muffley owned the Triumph Motorcycle Company, and to celebrate their eightieth birthdays, the Muffleys drove their Triumph motorcycles to McCook, Nebraska, and back.

It took only a week for the parsonage to be prepared for occupancy. Paul and Doris settled into a pretty two-bedroom red-brick home with rose bushes on two sides of the house.

WELCOME, LITTLE JANN

Within one month there was great news at the parsonage. Doris learned that baby number one was on the way.
In those days there was no ultrasound testing to find out
the sex of the baby, no glucose tolerance testing to see if a
mom's sugar count was too high, and no amniocentesis
testing to see if there would be the possibility of defects.
No, in 1959 the best advice to young mothers was "Try to
get off your feet a few times a day."

At 6:35 in the morning on September 24, 1959, a six-
pound, seven-ounce baby girl arrived. Paul and Doris
named their first child Jann Patricia Tassell. However, all
was not well. Doris hemorrhaged during delivery and
spent the next eight days in the hospital. After what
seemed like an eternity to the young family, the doctor
said Doris could go home. She had not been home long
when she hemorrhaged again and had to be rushed back
to the hospital. It was a tense time for the young couple,
and many people were bombarding the throne room of
Heaven on their behalf. The doctor did get the bleeding to
stop, and soon her strength began to rise. It was a great
relief and a great answer to prayer when Doris came
home from the hospital to stay.

ANOTHER GROWING BABY—BETHANY CHURCH

The Lord was blessing the new Bethany church. In
just a few months, the average attendance grew to 125 in
both the morning and evening services. At one of the first
meetings with the officers of the church, Tassell shared
his plans to convince the people that they were really Baptist. At the same time the General Association of Regular
Baptist Churches had fourteen literature items, which

were widely distributed to churches like Bethany that wanted the freedom of Biblical independence but also the benefits of fellowship with other believers of like precious faith. Dr. Paul introduced one of the literature items on the first Wednesday night of the month and then opened the meeting up for questions. That procedure took a total of fourteen months. In January 1960, at the annual business meeting, the church voted to change its name to Bethany Baptist Church. The church also voted to apply for fellowship with the General Association of Regular Baptist Churches. The vote that evening was thirty-two to three. The three wanted to hold on to their Congregational roots and traditions, but they graciously yielded to the will of the majority without causing any fuss. Bethany Baptist Church of Galesburg, Illinois, was on its way to becoming a strong lighthouse for Jesus Christ.

GOD'S PROVISION FOR GROWTH

Today it almost seems laughable that a church building seating 450 could be purchased for less than $50,000, yet that is what happened. The Swedish Covenant congregation decided to sell their downtown building and move to the suburbs, a decision that would again be a blessing to Bethany Baptist Church. Their asking price was $50,000. The building itself was located next to the Custer Hotel, one of the more popular places in town. Bethany Baptist offered the Covenant congregation $42,000, and they took it.

Dr. John R. Rice, through the *Sword of the Lord* newspaper, had been a positive source of information and influence on the people of Bethany Baptist Church. They decided to invite Dr. Rice to speak at the dedication service

of their new facilities. The church folk also invited the
Council of Ten of the Illinois-Missouri Association of
Regular Baptist Churches as their guests for the Sunday
afternoon festivities. The building was packed with more
than 450 people. One could feel the excitement and the
enthusiasm mounting as the people sang, accompanied
by an old-fashioned pipe organ and a new piano. Dr. Rice
preached a motivating message, encouraging the people
to use their new facilities for the glory of the Lord by win-
ning more souls to Christ. Everyone remembers it as a
great day in the history of Bethany Baptist Church.

By January 1961, Bethany Baptist was averaging just
under two hundred in the morning service. The teen
group averaged seventeen per Sunday, and six young
people had gone off to school at Bob Jones University.
Bethany was a young church with a young, energetic, and
fearless preacher. It was a good marriage between pastor
and church body, a marriage made, ordained, and blessed
in Heaven. In the heart of this young preacher burned a
growing, blazing fire for the souls of the men, women,
teenagers, and children of Galesburg. With each message
and with each moment spent in prayer, the burden on his
heart to reach people for Christ grew. God answered Dr.
Tassell's prayers and blessed him with many people to
reach.

NOTES

Opening Page: Charles C. Morrison, quoted by Cory, 67.

1. Lewis A. Drummond, *Spurgeon: Prince of Preachers* (Grand
   Rapids: Kregel Publications, 1992), 205.

CHAPTER SEVEN

The Crown of Rejoicing

The fruit of the righteous is a tree of life;
and he that winneth souls is wise.

PROVERBS 11:30

IT was September 1961 when Paul and Doris learned a second little bundle of joy was on the way. A few months later, the owner of the house the church rented and used as the parsonage decided to sell the house. The Tassells found a second-floor apartment with an outside entrance. The front door was at the top of thirteen steep steps. The number of trips spent walking up and down those steps hastened the arrival of their second daughter by eighteen days. On May 5, 1962, Jill Priscilla Tassell entered the world weighing a whopping six pounds and three ounces. No matter how many children one has, the birth of a baby is always new and certainly exciting. The same feelings come when one experiences new birth in Christ. The excitement of spiritual birth was seen countless times through the ministry of Dr. Paul.

AN "EASY BIRTH"

During his pastorate in Galesburg, Dr. Paul served on the board of directors of the Galesburg Rescue Mission. He also spoke at the mission on the first Monday night of each month. The service always closed with an invitation to receive Christ and a prayer. Then, at the end of the service, the mission superintendent lined the men up for beds and a good meal. While the men were waiting, Dr. Paul sat down at the piano and played stirring renditions of old hymns. One night in March 1963, a stout, curly haired man in his early forties staggered over to the piano and in slurring words asked, "Can you play 'How Great Thou Art'?"

Dr. Paul replied, "Yes, I can."

The drunk then responded, "You play, and I'll sing."

Dr. Paul went along, and to his utter amazement that hobo had a beautiful Irish/Italian tenor voice. By the time he got to the chorus, the man was sobbing and asked if he could speak to Dr. Paul the next day when he was sober. Tassell told him yes and explained that his office was at the church just four blocks away, next to the Hotel Custer. Dr. Paul said, "I'll see you at two o'clock tomorrow afternoon in my study," not really believing the intoxicated man would walk to a church building. Many promises like that have been made, only to be forgotten and broken the next day.

However, such was not the case this time. At 1:55 the next afternoon, there was a knock on Tassell's study door. There stood John Francis Cifelli, shaved, in clean clothes, and ready to talk. Dr. Paul said, "Have a seat, John, and tell me where you are from." Tassell almost fell off his chair when John said he had grown up in Toledo, Ohio. John had been born into a Roman Catholic family, but his parents abandoned him when he was six years old. His grandmother took him in and reared him. John started talking about Toledo and how a man by the name of Jess Fleck picked him up and took him to Sunday School at the Toledo Gospel Tabernacle. Jess Fleck was a dear friend of Paul Tassell's father! The elder Tassell often attended the men's Bible hour taught by Jess Fleck.

John also told Dr. Paul of his many experiences in the Navy during World War II. He had spent the years of 1945 and 1946 in the Veterans Administration Hospital trying to get relief from the constant pain in his body due to shrapnel lodged in his spine. He ultimately became an addict to alcohol and prescription drugs. John had spent the last seventeen years of his life wandering from one mission to another, desperately trying to keep body and soul together. By the end of his story, time had slipped by and Tassell had others waiting for him, so he suggested that John come back the next day at two o'clock. The next day at the appointed time John showed up again. Within fifteen minutes both Dr. Paul and John were on their knees as John prayed, expressing his trust in Christ as his personal Savior. Dr. Tassell personally discipled John and immersed him in the waters of baptism nine weeks later.

GOD'S WORK IN JOHN CIFELLI'S LIFE

One year later the mission superintendent retired. Tassell suggested that the rescue mission's board extend a call to John Francis Cifelli to be the next mission superintendent. The board agreed and voted favorably for John Cifelli to fill the office of superintendent of the mission. For the next two and a half years of his ministry in Galesburg, Tassell took John with him when he preached at youth rallies in the state. John sang "How Great Thou Art" and his personal favorite "Now I Belong to Jesus," after which Tassell presented a gospel message. There is no way to know how many teens were affected for Christ through the ministry team of Tassell and Cifelli. John Francis Cifelli died of a heart attack at the age of fifty-six.

Before John died, he flew back to Toledo to visit the aged Frank C. Cifelli, who had abandoned him years earlier. During the visit John led his father to Christ. John both sang and preached his father's funeral service. Also, before he died, the famous radio broadcast, *Unshackled,* from the Pacific Garden Mission, told the story of John Francis Cifelli.

A DIFFICULT BIRTH

Sometimes when the Lord draws a man or a woman to Himself, that person comes compliantly—broken and tearful, finally releasing him- or herself from the burden of sin and finding the freedom for which the soul had been desperately searching. Sometimes when the Lord draws a man or woman to Himself, that person comes kicking and screaming. That soul does not want to let go of the past, old habits, old friends, or the things he or she thought were enjoyable but that, in reality, had handcuffed the person to sin and the Devil's system. Perry Roger Shaw found himself in the latter category.

It was the first Sunday in January 1963 when one of the Sunday School bus children came to Tassell after the church service to tell him that her father was in St. Mary's Hospital with a bad case of gout. Her dad was notorious for his addiction to alcohol. The young girl was concerned about her father's spiritual condition, so she

asked her pastor to visit her dad in the hospital. Pastor
Tassell agreed to go.

On Monday afternoon Tassell walked the four blocks
to St. Mary's Hospital. Perry Shaw did not like Tassell,
nor did he want him or any other spiritual guru in his hospital room. The meeting that Monday with Shaw was brief
and filled with tension. Dr. Paul gave a quick plea for
Perry to receive Christ but was strongly rebuffed and told
he did not need any of what Tassell offered. Several
people put Perry Shaw on their prayer lists but saw nothing of him during the following months. Then something
happened that changed Perry Shaw forever.

Easter Sunday morning Pastor Tassell was just about
to sit down on the chair located behind the pulpit as the
service began. To his amazement he saw Perry Shaw, his
wife, son, and daughter filling up the better half of a pew.
At that moment Tassell asked the Lord to give him a message that would make the gospel of Jesus Christ clear and
tug at the heartstrings of Perry Shaw. The message
ended, the invitation hymn was played, but Perry Shaw
did not move. Pastor Tassell then called on one of the deacons to come and close the service in prayer so that he
could position himself to greet the Shaw family before
they could leave the church.

The Holy Spirit obviously had a hook in Perry Shaw
and was about to land him, because on the next Sunday,
Perry and his whole family showed up for church again. It
was Sunday, May 5, 1963, and the Tassell family was celebrating Jill Priscilla's first birthday. After the message,
Pastor Tassell gave the invitation, and Perry Shaw almost
ran down the aisle to receive Christ as his personal Savior.
He had been fighting God, trying desperately to suppress
the truth, but it had been a losing battle, and he couldn't

fight the convicting power of the Holy Spirit any longer. He gave his heart to Christ and realized for the first time that Jesus came to free us of our sin, not to keep us from having a good time. After several weeks of personal discipleship, Pastor Tassell baptized Perry Roger Shaw and he became a member of Bethany Baptist Church.

CELEBRATING A BIRTHDAY

Ever since that day Perry Shaw has called Pastor Tassell on May 5, the anniversary date of his salvation. Every year when Pastor Tassell picks up the phone, Perry Roger Shaw shouts, "Praise the Lord, Dr. Paul!" and then he says, "Thank you for leading me to Christ." Perry has served the Lord as a Sunday School teacher and a deacon of Bethany Baptist Church, and he continues to grow and prosper spiritually. Needless to say, John F. Cifelli and Perry Roger Shaw became good friends and served the Lord together at Bethany Baptist Church.

FREED FROM A CULT

There is an inexplicable power when the Word of God is preached with passion. The writer of Hebrews tells us that the Word of God is as sharp as a two-edged sword that cuts all the way down to the intentions of the heart. It peels back all our rationalizations and exposes our feeble excuses for not loving and following Jesus. Many men have tried to discredit, change, and even destroy the Word of God, but that is an impossible task. One such man was Charles Taze Russell, founder of the cult called Jehovah's Witnesses. This man, energized by the Devil himself, wrote his own version of so-called divine revelation and in doing so has led multiplied thousands of people to Hell. One man caught in this deceptive trap lived in Galesburg, Illinois. His name was John Nelson. Dr. Tassell was preaching the Word of God in a publicly announced series that would expose the cults as nothing but lies from the pit of Hell. Unbeknown to Dr. Tassell, John Nelson, a leader in the Galesburg Kingdom Hall, decided he would attend the series and try to discredit Tassell's teaching.

A year passed after Dr. Paul had preached that series of messages on the cults, and the Word of God was slowly performing surgery on John Nelson's heart. One Saturday morning the tall, lanky, almost gaunt man sat down in Dr. Paul's office. With quivering lips he finally introduced himself as one of the leaders of the Jehovah's Witnesses in town. Nelson asked Tassell if he recalled the sermon series, especially the night he preached on the Jehovah's Witnesses.

"I was so angry at you that night," said Nelson, "that I wanted to call you outside and punch your lights out. However, just before you closed the service, you gave one last challenge to any in the room who might be Jehovah's Witnesses: 'Read through the entire New Testament, for you will discover that Charles Russell was terribly wrong. You will discover that Jesus Christ is Jehovah, and you will have to yield to His way of salvation.' "

At that point in the conversation, John Nelson's body began to shake. He could control his emotions no longer, and the dam holding back his tears burst into a torrent of sobs. Through the tears and with a cracking voice, Nelson choked out, "I took you up on that challenge to prove you wrong, but after reading the Gospel of John, I realized I was the one who was wrong, and I need Jesus to be my Savior." Both men immediately fell on their knees. Both wept as John Nelson humbly sobbed his way into the loving arms of Jesus.

Dr. Paul baptized John Nelson and he joined Bethany Baptist Church. Nelson later moved to another state, but instead of being a cult member, he was a sinner saved by the grace of God through faith in Jesus Christ.

"HOT STUFF"

Pride is a dangerous sin, for it can keep a man out of Heaven and take him straight to Hell. Ellis Wells, a Galesburg businessman, was a pompous, self-righteous man with a problem: he was on his way to Hell. His wife and daughter, who were true Christians, loved Ellis very much and prayed for him daily. Ellis came to Bethany Baptist Church occasionally to please his wife or to hear his daughter sing.

Late one Sunday afternoon Ellis Wells was rushed to the hospital. Pastor Tassell received a call and went immediately to see Wells. Upon arriving at the nurses' station, Tassell learned that they were preparing Ellis for an emergency appendectomy. When Tassell walked into the hospital room, he found a man who was no longer proud but beginning to understand the frailty of human life. Ellis Wells was literally trembling under the convicting power of the Holy Spirit. He begged Tassell to lead him to Christ. Right there on that hospital bed, with the tears flowing, Ellis Wells gave his heart to Jesus.

Pastor Tassell was already late for the evening service, so he ran out of the hospital and drove like a junior Jehu to the church building. Pulling into the parking lot, he slammed the gear shift into park, jumped out of the car, and ran into the church. One of the deacons standing inside the door asked if he could do anything to help, and Tassell replied, "Just let me preach!" Approximately two hours later, Dr. Paul went back to the parking lot only to discover to his chagrin that the engine was still running! But Ellis Wells had become a child of God, and that was worth so much more than a hot engine and a tank of gasoline.

A CROWN OF REJOICING

Galesburg, Illinois, was the birthplace of Carl Sandburg, Abraham Lincoln's biographer. In 1915, Ronald Reagan's family moved to Galesburg, where he attended the Silas Willard School. Galesburg was a stronghold for Lutheranism, and many people were steeped in strong liturgy and tradition. However, Dr. Paul Tassell discovered that faithful, relentless, personal evangelism is the best way to win lost yet religious people to Christ. Starting with the faithful few in November 1959, Bethany Baptist Church experienced steady if not dramatic numerical and spiritual growth. When Dr. Paul left Bethany, the average Sunday School attendance was 240. People were being saved, baptized, and discipled. Marriages and families were being strengthened, and Christians were enjoying true fellowship. Men like John Francis Cifelli, Perry Roger Shaw, John Nelson, and Ellis Wells, along with many others, will one day stand with Pastor Tassell before the Lord as a "Crown of Rejoicing."

MORE CHANGES

Two seemingly small circumstances took place while Paul and Doris served the Lord in Galesburg. One was a family matter, and the other was a shift in ministry emphasis. Both would have ramifications on their future.

It was while Dr. Paul was ministering in Galesburg that his father, Albert Tassell, Sr., received bad news from the doctor. For many years the elder Tassell had suffered with chronic bronchitis. The doctor told him his lungs were permanently damaged and that he would probably not survive another winter in Toledo, Ohio. He was only fifty-five years old, and he had spent his entire adult life in Toledo working primarily as an insurance salesman. Dr. Paul's dad immediately began looking for a job in the drier regions of the western part of the United States. He found that employment in Las Vegas, Nevada. When the Tassells moved there in 1962, it was a relatively small town of fifty thousand people. It is now a bustling metropolis of more than a million. Mr. Tassell worked there until a heart attack took him to Heaven in 1973.

Jerry, Dr. Paul's kid brother, was thirteen years old when the family moved west. After his father's death, Jerry continued to live with and look after his mother until her death in November 1994. Jerry, a bachelor, still resides in Las Vegas.

It was also at this time in Dr. Paul's life that he began to place a greater emphasis on ministering to and discipling young people. He and Doris put Jann and Jill in their strollers, met the teens at the church, and walked two miles to the park. There they played ball, ate a picnic lunch, and had a devotional time in the Word of God. It was a great time for Dr. Paul and Doris to model authentic Christianity and influence teens for the cause of Christ.

One of those young people was John Carlson. He was the first young man called into the ministry under Dr. Paul's leadership. John went off to Bob Jones University to study for the ministry. God would lead John back to

Galesburg, where he now pastors Bethany Baptist Church. Working with those young people was significant. God had plans for the Tassells' future that would include national youth leadership, ministering in camps and on college campuses across the country. Dr. Paul's preparation in Galesburg was vital for what lay ahead.

The old gospel song "I'll Go Where You Want Me to Go, Dear Lord," began to take on new meaning. The Lord began to stir up an unsettled feeling in the soul of Dr. Paul. On the one hand he believed he might stay in Galesburg the entire length of his ministry, yet on the other hand he realized God might want him to move on to a new ministry. He was certain of one thing though: that God would lead him and he would follow.

Campus Baptist Church, Ames, Iowa

Don't be afraid of size. I encourage pastors, when the Lord for some reason chooses you to be part of a movement where growth, His kind of multiplying growth, occurs, don't fight it. Now, don't manipulate it. Don't act as though you're responsible for it. But you have to respond to it just like a family.

CHUCK SWINDOLL

HERODOTUS wrote, "There is nothing permanent but change."[1] From November 1958 to January 1964, Dr. Tassell had received no contacts from any pulpit committees. But that was about to change. Dr. Paul Jackson, the national representative of the General Association of Regular Baptist Churches, wrote to Tassell advising him that he had recommended him to the pulpit committee of Campus Baptist Church in Ames, Iowa, hometown of Iowa State University. Dr. Tassell had his first taste of campus evangelism in Galesburg at Knox College. Rev. John Blanchard became president of the school in 1845 and later led Wheaton College in Wheaton, Illinois. Unfortunately, Knox College could no longer even be remotely classified as a fundamentalist institution. Dr. Tassell found it exciting to go on the campus and talk to the students about Christ. It sparked an evangelistic flame in his heart for young people.

Two weeks after receiving the letter from Dr. Jackson, Dr. Tassell received a telephone call from Vernard Whattoff, the chairman of the pulpit committee of Campus Baptist Church. Whattoff invited Tassell to come to Campus Baptist, but Tassell told him that everything was fine at Bethany Baptist Church and that he felt no compulsion to even think about leaving.

A PERSISTENT PASTORAL SEARCH COMMITTEE

One Sunday morning Bethany Baptist had an unusual number of visitors. Bob Swanson, chairman of the deacon board, passed a note from the choir loft to Dr. Tassell during the offering. The note read, "I smell a pulpit committee." Actually, three pulpit committees were there that day, but the men from Iowa were the most persistent! In early February Tassell received a large packet of materials telling him about Campus Baptist Church. The church had a two-pronged outreach. The first was on the campus of Iowa State University, and the second was in the Ames community as a whole.

Brother Whattoff called again a week after Tassell had received the packet of information. However, Tassell reiterated that he had no peace about giving up the ministry in Galesburg. To Tassell's amazement Whattoff called again in March and again in April, and then again in May. The men at Campus Baptist believed that Dr. Paul Tassell was the man God had for the pulpit in Ames, and they were serious in communicating that belief to him.

In June 1964, the GARBC Annual Conference met at Winona Lake, Indiana, in the famed Billy Sunday Tabernacle, which held more than five thousand people. Dr. Tassell had the rare privilege as a twenty-nine-year-old preacher to bring the Bible message Friday morning. After he finished preaching, he stepped off the platform to find six people waiting to talk with him. Two of the men were Dr. Ernest Pickering and Dr. Bryce Augsburger. They wanted to speak with him about becoming more involved with the GARBC. The other four men were pulpit committee members from Campus Baptist Church of Ames, Iowa.

A SLEEPLESS NIGHT

After talking with the pulpit committee through the lunch hour, Dr. Tassell was still unconvinced that he should leave Bethany Baptist Church. The conference ended, but the pulpit committee persisted in extending the call to Dr. Tassell. Vernard Whattoff called back in July, August, September, October, and November. Then something happened during the Thanksgiving holiday that changed the course of Dr. Tassell's life.

He was the guest speaker at a statewide youth rally in Moline, Illinois. As usual, Dr. Tassell was running a tight schedule, preaching also that week at an evangelistic campaign in Peoria, Illinois, about a two-hour drive from Moline. Friday night he got away as soon as possible from Peoria and headed for Moline, arriving at the Holiday Inn about midnight. He was scheduled to speak at nine o'clock the next morning to several hundred teenagers.

That night Dr. Tassell could not sleep. Frustrated and
a little bit anxious, he got out of his bed just after one
o'clock, fell to his knees, and prayed, "Lord, I have to
preach eight hours from now, and I desperately need
some rest. I promise I will call Vernard Whattoff as soon
as I finish preaching tomorrow morning." Tassell crawled
back into bed and slept soundly.

Shortly before noon Dr. Tassell picked up the telephone and dialed Vernard Whattoff's number. Tassell
started the conversation with, "I suppose, Brother
Whattoff, you have called a man by now."

The chairman replied, "As a matter of fact, Dr. Paul,
we had a special prayer meeting for you last night which
lasted until almost one o'clock."

Paul Tassell said, "I surrender!"

Knowing God's will does not magically make it easier
to leave the people you love. Dr. Tassell had been
Bethany Baptist Church's first pastor. There were many
new believers growing in Christ as a result of Dr. Paul's
ministry. The people did not want to see their pastor go.
The night when Dr. Tassell informed the deacons and
trustees of his decision to candidate at Campus Baptist in
Iowa, he called on Bob Swanson to pray for the wisdom
he needed to know God's will. Brother Swanson replied,
"No, Dr. Paul, I can't pray about that. No one here wants
you to leave." But God's mercy and grace would be suffi-
cient to mend their broken hearts and ease their minds
about where He was leading their pastor.

On December 13, 1964, Dr. Tassell and Doris officially
candidated at Campus Baptist Church in Ames, Iowa. On
December 16, the congregation voted eighty-eight to zero
to call Dr. Paul Tassell to be their pastor. On an extremely
cold day in February 1965, Doris moved the family into

their new tri-level home in Ames, Iowa. Paul stayed behind to preach his last Sunday in Galesburg. Dr. Paul and Doris have often remarked about how difficult it was to say good-bye to the people God had allowed them to minister to.

It was time to look ahead to Ames, Iowa, and Campus Baptist Church. Paul and Doris have often referred to those years in Iowa as the "Glory Years."

NOTES

Opening Page: Charles R. Swindoll, *The Tale of the Tardy Oxcart* (Nashville: Word Publishing, 1998), 92.

1. Herodotus, quoted by Zuck, 47.

The Glory Years

. . . I will build my church; and the gates of hell
shall not prevail against it.

MATTHEW 16:18

D R. Tassell's predecessor at Campus Baptist was Pastor Milton Dowden. He had led the church through a rather stormy building program, which meant that Tassell preached in a new auditorium with seating for five hundred. He immediately went to work on emphasizing the preaching and teaching of God's Word. "Just let me preach," and the Word of God by the power of the Holy Spirit will bring the increase.

Within just a few short months Campus Baptist Church saw significant growth both in the community outreach and on the campus of Iowa State University. It was not long before scores of college students were coming to hear the young preacher expound the Word of God. His zeal and his enthusiasm for the Bible were something most of the students had never seen. Many of them came from liberal Methodist, Presbyterian, and Baptist congregations. They were used to seeing and feeling an icicle in the pulpit, but now they were experiencing something totally different. They were hearing, many for the first time, a Spirit-filled, Bible-centered message. They also learned that the Bible is the Word of God, that God's Word is truth, and the truth was exactly what those students were looking for and needed.

A YOUNG MAN ON A MISSION

At the same time a cultural revolution was taking place in the United States. It was stimulated by a number of climates and events. Some of these included the assassinations of President John F. Kennedy, his brother Robert Kennedy, and Martin Luther King, Jr.; the Kinsey Report, which added fire to the free love movement by falsely documenting the supposed sexual habits and desires of men and women; and, of course, the police action in a small faraway place called Vietnam. The United States sat fractured. Political activism and civil rebellion became common. Sit-ins on college campuses, protest marches in the streets, and the daily death count from Vietnam were the regular features on the nightly news. Yes, the young people were looking for truth. Where would they find it? For many of the students at Iowa State University the truth was found at Campus Baptist Church.

One of those students not only knew the truth but also practiced it, a young man by the name of Larry Bleeker. Larry graduated from ISU in the spring of 1967. During his five years of undergraduate and graduate studies, he led sixty of his ISU friends to saving faith in Jesus Christ. Even at the early age of twenty-four, Larry Bleeker was a master soul winner. He was part of the college quartet, a fine athlete, and the epitome of a Christian soldier. In the summer of 1967, Larry went to Dr. Paul's study to inform him that he intended to enlist in the United States Marine Corps. Larry said, "The toughest men in the world are Marines, and I want to win the toughest men in the world to Christ." Dr. Paul tried to talk him out of enlisting, but Larry Bleeker was determined this was God's will for his life.

After basic training Bleeker was commissioned a second lieutenant in the Third Marine Division and sent to Vietnam on October 1, 1967. Fifteen days later on October 16, 1967, a sniper put a bullet through Larry Bleeker's head.

Campus Baptist Church was packed for the funeral. Five hundred fifty people attended Larry Bleeker's memorial service. Three television stations covered the service. When Dr. Paul gave the invitation to receive Christ, three young men answered the call. Larry Bleeker was buried with full military honors, which cannot compare to the rewards he will receive in Heaven. "For to me to live is Christ, and to die is gain," wrote the apostle Paul to the Philippian church. That verse truly characterized Larry's life. At a young age and even in death he was a Christlike example to the believers.

NO PLACE FOR RACISM IN TASSELL'S CHURCH

Another event that threatened the peace and stirred the people of ISU and the citizens of Ames was the assassination of Dr. Martin Luther King, Jr. The angry feelings of the African-American students threatened to explode with destructive violence. On the morning after the assassination, Dr. Tassell decided to call Ezell Wiggins, pastor of the True Bible Baptist Church in Des Moines, Iowa.

Pastor Wiggins was a longtime, experienced Black pastor
and counselor. Tassell and Wiggins brought together
many of the Black students on the ISU campus for a time
of quiet Bible study, discussion on the news of the assassination and what the response should be, and prayer. Dr.
Paul said later, "God used Pastor Wiggins to save Ames
from terrible rioting and violence." Others noted that the
wise counsel of Wiggins and Tassell helped avert tragedy
in Ames, Iowa, that week.

Unfortunately the ugly face of racism rears its head
even in evangelical circles. If it is not squashed immediately, it will cause division and eventually kill a church. One
Sunday morning Dr. Paul was sitting at his desk when one
of the men of the church stopped by to comment on the
nominations for the different offices of the church, including head usher. He said, "If that nigger gets elected as the
head usher, then I'm leaving the church." Dr. Tassell immediately stood up, locked his steely blue eyes onto the
eyes of the other man, and said, "Good-bye."

The godly Black man was elected head usher. The
man who threatened to leave repented of his sin and
stayed. In fact, the two men became good friends. That
Black man was Frank Gainer, who later graduated from
ISU with a Ph.D. in chemistry. Just recently Dr. Gainer retired after a distinguished career with the Lily Pharma-
ceutical Company.

AN ADJUSTMENT IN MINISTRY STYLE

Campus Baptist Church was truly an integrated
church. During his ministry, Tassell baptized into the
membership African-Americans, Asians, Ghanians, and
Nigerians. Many people from all over the world, with vari-

ous backgrounds and family histories, gathered at Campus Baptist Church to worship the one true God. One of the reasons Dr. Paul was able to exert such a great deal of influence in the lives of so many people, even international students, was his God-given ability to adjust his ministry style without a long-term transition. In Elberton and Galesburg, which were smaller in numbers of people, Tassell combined strong Bible preaching with close personal ties and one-on-one discipleship. Moving to a larger work with the potential of reaching many more people in Ames, Dr. Paul shifted the way he ministered. He realized that to reach more people with the gospel of Jesus Christ his priorities would have to be preaching, writing, working with the deacons, and building a quality staff. Others would then be responsible for the one-on-one discipleship and care ministries.

IMPACTING STUDENTS

Another reason Dr. Paul had such an impact on the students at ISU was that for almost two years he had been going to the dormitories at the invitation of some of the students for question-and-answer times on Bible subjects. Sometimes these sessions lasted until midnight. Many of the students who sat in on those sessions came to church the next Sunday and trusted Christ as Savior. Dr. Paul always encouraged the Campus Baptist students to be bold witnesses for Christ to their roommates and friends on campus.

Hal Miller was pastoring at this time in Iowa Falls. Dr. Paul and Hal began circulating among the students at Ellsworth College. Their fruitful campus outreach eventually gave birth to Campus Bible Fellowship, a college ministry that Miller presented to Baptist Mid-Missions in 1965. Through the years, Campus Bible Fellowship has reached untold numbers of college students for Christ, with a worldwide impact by ministering to international students.

A LASTING INFLUENCE

Campus Baptist Church saw unprecedented growth during Dr. Paul's ministry. By the time he had completed his service as pastor, the church had grown to more than six hundred, which necessitated double services. He also looked for quality guest speakers and missionaries to expose the church to worldwide ministry.

One such man and his wife were Bob and Mary Smith, longtime missionaries to Liberia. The Smiths had to leave the mission field because of Mary's poor health. Bob felt led of the Lord to go into full-time evangelistic work in the United States. He was one of the most powerful preachers Tassell had ever heard. His messages were captivating with his many stories of Africa, wild beasts, and satanic religions.

Campus Baptist Church decided to call Bob Smith for a twelve-day evangelistic crusade. It began on Wednesday night and lasted through two Sundays. After the first meeting no one worried about attendance. The college students were hooked, and the Lord worked mightily in scores of lives. When the campaign was over, the church had registered 101 public decisions for Christ. Most of those decisions were made by college students who today are pastors, missionaries, and Christian schoolteachers scattered all over the world serving Christ. Bob and Mary Smith have both gone Home to be with the Lord, but they are not forgotten.

Little Paul (left)

Paul (left) with his mother and paternal grandparents;
brother, Al; sisters, Ruth Ann and Barbara

With some friends

Early teen years

Studying in dorm room at BJU

Doris and Paul at BJU graduation

Pastor Tassell holding youngest parishioner in Elberton, Georgia

Thirty years old in Galesburg, Illinois

*Dr. Paul giving right hand of fellowship to
new members of Campus Baptist, Ames, Iowa*

*Pastor Tassell greeting folks in lobby of
Campus Baptist Church*

Pastoring in Ames

National youth representative of GARBC

In front of Wise Active Youth display with son, Joseph

Playing the piano

Preacher brothers, Al and Paul Tassell

*Family at time of move to
Des Moines, Iowa*

*Groundbreaking for
educational building
at Grandview Park
Baptist in Des Moines*

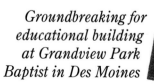

Familiar photo while national representative of GARBC

*Receiving doctor of letters at Cedarville College
(now Cedarville University)*

Paul helps clean recreation building at a camp

*Visiting new church building
in Avon Park, Florida*

In the airport at Kodiak Island, Alaska

With Paul Levin at Bill Rice Ranch, 1988

Guess where they've been!

*Proud grandpa with Jordan,
first grandchild*

Just let me preach!

Receiving Medal of Honor—Cedarville, 1994
From left, Paul, Doris, and President Paul Dixon

*Flag plaque awarded by chaplains
at GARBC Annual Conference,
Bellevue, Washington, 1994*

Nate and Jill help celebrate Paul's retirement

*The Tassell family at Faith Baptist Church, Winter Haven,
Florida—celebrating fifty years of preaching,
January 22, 2000*

THE BABY AND THE GARAGE DOOR

The most memorable event that took place at Campus Baptist Church for the Tassell family was the birth of their third child. Joseph Paul was born on August 17, 1966. Dr. Paul was very excited and could not wait for the next Sunday to arrive so he could show off his new son. The day finally came, and he helped get the girls into the car, which was parked in the garage. Then, like a gentleman should, he assisted Doris into the car and handed her the baby. This was long before car seats were mandatory. Tassell then slid in behind the steering wheel, started the engine, put the car into reverse, and backed right through the garage door. The ghastly noises of glass shattering, wood snapping, and steel scraping horrified the family inside the car. Their Catholic neighbor, Patrick Burns, came running across the street to see if everyone was all right. He then offered the Tassells his beat-up old Ford to go to church. Burns assured Tassell that he had already been to mass! They decided to pull the car back into the garage, which created even more noise. When Dr. Paul drove up to church in that old Ford, the people began to wonder why he was not driving his brand-new Chevy. Of course, there was no way for the preacher to avoid the truth. Soon the story spread like wildfire through the congregation. The Tassell home had a large picture window, and Dr. Paul sat there all afternoon as car after car of church people drove by and stopped for a few minutes of uncontrolled laughter.

WHERE IS PASTOR?

Campus Baptist Church was situated right across the street from Iowa State University and just a short drive

from Faith Baptist Bible College in the town of Ankeny.
Naturally, Dr. Paul performed many weddings during his
years there. At some weddings the bride or groom might
show up a bit late, but on this particular day the preacher
almost did not show up at all.

Two of Dr. Tassell's best friends throughout his years
of ministry were evangelist Paul Levin and his musical associate, a blind singer named Bob Findley. Paul Levin
spent his summer months speaking to the teens at the
Bill Rice Ranch. Bob Findley, therefore, had eight or nine
weeks with no singing engagements, so Tassell invited
Findley to Campus Baptist Church for a Saturday night
and Sunday concert. Tassell told Findley he would pick
him up at his home in Cedar Rapids at nine o'clock on Saturday morning and they would easily make it back to
Ames in time for the pastor to get cleaned up and dressed
for a two o'clock wedding. However, on the way home on
a hilly stretch of the highway, the car was involved in an
unavoidable collision.

Fortunately no one was badly injured, but by the time
the tow truck came and the state trooper had filled out his
report, it was almost two o'clock, and they were still sixty
miles from the church.

By then the church was comfortably full. Juanita
Boylan sat down at the organ and began to play what she
thought was going to be a fifteen-minute prelude. In the
meantime the deacons were in the back of the church
frantically trying to find Dr. Paul. Cell phones didn't exist
back then, and no one answered the door at the parsonage. By 2:30, Mrs. Boylan had been playing the organ for
almost forty-five minutes. The state trooper took Tassell
home, where he showered, shaved, and put on a suit. He
finally arrived at the church at 2:50. Juanita Boylan was

exhausted. Tassell told the people he would explain what happened after the wedding.

These two incidents will never be forgotten by the Tassell family or by the church people. Whenever Dr. Paul meets people from Ames, Iowa, it is not long before someone brings up the garage door or the parson who was late for the wedding.

PREACH, PREACH, PREACH

Sometimes the life of a busy pastor just gets busier. Along with the administration of a growing church, an outreach to the students on college campuses, and an expanding family, Tassell was becoming more and more sought after as a guest speaker for summer camps and youth rallies. He had a way of connecting with young people, which gave the Holy Spirit incredible freedom to work in their hearts and change their lives. His messages were straight from the Bible with alliterated outlines that were easy to remember. He was always full of humor, and the young people loved to be around him. His jokes were corny, but just the way he told them made people laugh. But when it came to salvation, getting one's life right with God, or being called to the Lord's work, Tassell considered that serious business. One is either the child of God, or one is not. One either lives for God, or one does not. There is no middle ground, and one cannot have it both ways, he would tell the young people. Hundreds of them responded to the convicting work of the Holy Spirit. "Just let me preach!" shouted Dr. Paul from the tips of his toes, and the Lord harvested the fruit.

The young preachers of our day need to step back and take a lesson from the past. Solomon said there is nothing

new under the sun, and that goes for preaching the Word
of God. History tells us that God uses men who, without
hesitation and without apology, stand up and preach
God's Word. Passionate expository preaching that
reaches into the soul and makes that person face the
truth about him- or herself, about the world, and about
the true God of the Bible is the only thing that will genuinely grow a church and start a revival in the hearts of
people. That is what Dr. Paul Norman Tassell endeavored
to do with his life for fifty fruitful years.

KEEPING UP THE PACE

The college students at Iowa State University challenged Dr. Paul in many ways. Paul was only thirty-one
years old, but he realized he would need to begin a regular exercise routine to keep his body in good physical
condition so he could keep up with those college kids.
One form of exercise Paul enjoyed was jumping rope. He
spent many hours building leg strength and endurance
jumping rope in his garage. Across the street from the
church was the college track. One of the college students,
David Powell, challenged Dr. Paul to jog in order to increase his stamina. David offered to run with him, and
soon all the students recognized Dr. Paul on the track.
They even presented him with a T-shirt with the following
inscription on the back: "You've just been passed by the
world's shortest jogger." These activities endeared Dr.
Paul to the students and gave him many opportunities to
share Jesus Christ with them.

Doris kept the home fires burning. The children were
young and demanded most of her attention. She was able
to teach a Sunday School class, and she always worked in

the Vacation Bible School. On one occasion Doris and several other ladies went to minister at the girls' detention center. When Doris gave the invitation, sixty girls came forward to receive Christ. The warden was not pleased that it took so long, but the ladies dealt with each girl individually.

If someone were to have tried to keep pace with this young preacher, they would have quit from exhaustion. Paul Tassell was driven by a sixth sense of urgency, which seemed to push him to accomplish more for Christ. It was as if he somehow knew his time would prematurely run out. So he was consumed with preaching, visiting, debating the social issues of the day, administrating a church, and writing. He was in the prime of his life. He was in peak physical shape. He was a frontline soldier in God's army. He found contentment being in the heat of the battle. He would not sit on the sidelines. He would competently and confidently lead others into the fray and guide them to victory, teaching them to trust Christ. Mistakes? There were many, but he would not allow them to dictate his life. Hurts? Of course, but there was not enough time to allow emotion to get in the way. These were the years God had given him to spread the light of the gospel, and he would do it with all his might.

CHAPTER TEN

Contending for
the Faith

*Put it before them briefly, so they will read it, clearly so they will
appreciate it, picturesquely so they will remember it, and
above all, accurately so they will be guided by its light.*

JOSEPH PULITZER

PAUL Tassell was a fervent,
faithful, fearless fighter for
the faith. This was evident
in his preaching, as well as through his prolific pen.
While in Galesburg, he had been elected to the Council
of Ten in Illinois. While serving in that position, he became the editor of the *IL/MO Trumpet,* the state paper
of the Illinois-Missouri Association of Regular Baptist
Churches. In 1966, Regular Baptist Press (RBP) published Tassell's book titled *Secrets of the Blessed Man.* In
1967, RBP published his *Contemporary Outlines from
Isaiah,* and in 1968, he wrote *Outline Studies of Jeremiah.*
But the one event that catapulted Dr. Paul into the position of the leading "evangelical" in Ames, especially on

the campuses of Iowa State University and Faith Baptist Bible College, was his response to Stanley Borden, pastor of First Baptist Church in Ames. During the Christmas season of 1969, Borden preached and then published in the *Ames Daily Tribune* his message that cast doubt on the virgin birth of Christ. (See Addendum I for Dr. Borden's message as it appeared in the newspaper, as well as Dr. Tassell's response.)

Benjamin Franklin once said, "If you would not be forgotten as soon as you are dead, either write things worth reading, or do things worth writing."[1] In his life, Paul Tassell has accomplished both. Shepherding churches, which significantly changed the lives of people, ultimately resulted in altering the course of a community. In picking up his pen, Tassell left a legacy and model for young preachers to study.

In 1978, Dr. Tassell wrote *Sweeter Than Honey*, which is now in its fourth printing. In 1983, he wrote *Pathways to Power*. In 1991, and in the beginning stages of Parkinson's disease, he wrote a 423-page history of the General Association of Regular Baptist Churches titled *Quest for Faithfulness*. In that volume he wrote about the men, the churches, and the events that shaped the GARBC of today. In the years to come he would author numerous additional articles and pamphlets and sermons, articulately defending the authority of the Bible and encouraging Christians to maintain graceful balance in their Christian walk.

Donald Demaray wrote, "All [great preachers] are writers. The alert preacher will be certain to print that literature from his ministry which can be of help to others."[2] It can be said with certainty that Dr. Paul Tassell has been a blessing to others by the prolific use of his pen.

A LOVE OF READING

"All great preachers are eager students possessed of an insatiable desire to read and gather information. . . . Wesley insisted his preachers study several hours daily; of those who had no taste for study, he demanded that they develop it."[3]

Dr. Tassell was a man who loved to read. He has told many young preachers, "If you do not read, you will dry up, and your preaching will become dusty."

He was a friend of books. He read constantly. Besides devouring religious books of all kinds, he especially enjoyed reading biographies. By studying the lives of great men, he found material to benefit his life and teaching.

Many times he said that John A. Broadus had written the greatest commentary on the book of Matthew. He read and studied this six-hundred-page commentary twice. He also read and studied through the seventeen-volume commentary of the whole Bible by B. H. Carroll, titled *An Interpretation of the English Bible.*

Dr. Tassell is a firm believer in every Bible student having a good commentary on the book of Revelation. He believes that the 381 pages of outline studies by Lehman Strauss, published by Loizeaux Brothers, Neptune, New Jersey, is the best.

A MAN OF PASSION

Vance Havner observed, "A preacher may be wrapped in the robes of learning, and his study walls may be decked with diplomas. His home may be filled with travel souvenirs from many lands, and he may wear all the trappings of ecclesiastical prestige and pageantry. But he cannot function without unction."[4]

Preaching was the lifeblood of Dr. Paul Tassell. People found it difficult to fall asleep when he preached. His clear voice seemed to make the messages come alive. His alliterated sermons made it easy for one to take notes and to remember the outlines of the passages he preached. (In Addendum II, you will find the outlines to some of Dr. Tassell's favorite sermons.)

John Walvoord once commented at a seminary graduation, "I'm afraid for this class—that we are turning out too many graduates who have a great number of beliefs but not enough conviction."[5] Paul Tassell became known as a man of conviction. His preaching and his lifestyle soundly demonstrate that he could be counted as a separated, fundamental Baptist. On November 6–9, 1978, Paul, along with other fundamentalists such as J. Don Jennings, Charles Wagner, Wendell Zimmerman, James Jeremiah, Wendell Kempton, and Bob Jones, Jr., met at Temple Baptist Church in Detroit, Michigan, for the Sixth Fundamental Baptist Congress of North America. Thousands gathered to hear the great fundamental doctrines of the faith fervently preached. Paul Tassell's subject for that meeting was the Second Coming of Christ. His text was Acts 1:9–11. (You will find the outline of that message in Addendum II.)

A LOVE OF MUSIC

Almost any church service includes some type of music played or sung. Dr. Tassell loves music. He played the piano and the violin. He loves hundreds of hymns and gospel songs. Some of his favorites include "I'd

Rather Have Jesus," "The Love of God," "All Hail the
Power of Jesus' Name," "Under His Wings," and "Jesus
Loves Even Me." Paul found it difficult to single out one
gospel song as his all-time favorite; however, he is espe-
cially fond of the third stanza of "It Is Well with My
Soul."

> My sin—O the bliss of this glorious tho't—
> My sin, not in part, but the whole,
> Is nailed to the cross, and I bear it no more:
> Praise the Lord, Praise the Lord, O my soul.
> — *Horatio G. Spafford*

HE STOOD TALL

Reading the Word of God and other great books, writing what God had put on his heart, singing great gospel
songs loaded with praise and rich theology, and preaching powerful messages from the Bible that the Holy Spirit
used to bring about change in the hearts of people—that
was Dr. Paul Tassell's life. It was simple and straight-
forward, yet filled with, and under the unction of, the
Holy Spirit. There is always something inexplicable about
a life energized by the Holy Spirit. When one looks at
Paul Tassell, one does not see a mountain of a man who
can intimidate by his sheer size. Nor will one find an intellectual genius on the level of Albert Einstein. One will not
find a man who has amassed a great fortune like Bill
Gates. But one will find a humble, hardworking man who
had an intense desire to allow God to use him in unique
ways in the lives of other people. Although Dr. Tassell
was only five feet seven inches in height, he stood tall on
the Word of God in contending for the faith.

NOTES

Opening Page: Joseph Pulitzer, quoted by Zuck, 426.

1. Benjamin Franklin, quoted by Zuck, 427.

2. Donald E. Demaray, *Pulpit Giants* (Chicago: Moody Press, 1973), 166.

3. Demaray, 166

4. Vance Havner, quoted by George Sweeting, compiler, *Who Said That?* (Chicago: Moody Press, 1994), 365.

5. John Walvoord, quoted by Swindoll, 421.

National Youth Representative

*Let no man despise thy youth; but be thou an example of the
believers, in word, in conversation, in charity,
in spirit, in faith, in purity.*

1 TIMOTHY 4:12

I N May 1969, Paul R. Jackson went Home to be with the Lord. He had served as the national representative of the General Association of Regular Baptist Churches since 1960. Dr. Joseph M. Stowell succeeded Dr. Jackson in June 1969. Dr. Stowell initiated a weekly radio broadcast and chose William Kuhnle as his assistant in charge of the radio ministry. Dr. Stowell also had a burden for the youth of the GARBC fellowship.

"YOU'RE THE MAN"

Dr. Tassell had been elected to the GARBC national Council of Fourteen. The council met twice a year—in

101

December and then in June just before the annual conference. At the December 1969 meeting of the council, Dr.
Stowell took Dr. Tassell home with him instead of letting
him check into the hotel like the other council members.
For a couple of hours before going to bed, Dr. Stowell out-
lined for Tassell his conviction that it was time for the
GARBC to have a national youth director.

As pastor of a church that ministered successfully to
scores of high school and college students, Dr. Paul was
increasingly asked to speak at youth rallies, camp meetings, and summer camps. These invitations did not go unnoticed by others in the Fellowship, including Dr. Stowell.
It was his conviction that Tassell was the man God wanted
to fill the role of national youth representative.

After the Council of Fourteen meetings ended, Tassell
headed to Chicago's O'Hare Airport with mixed emotions. He had been in Ames only four years, and the blessing of God was obviously on his ministry there. Despite
Dr. Stowell's persuasive and persistent presentation,
Tassell finally decided to decline his offer.

Both Dr. Merle R. Hull, the executive editor of Regular Baptist Press, and Dr. Stowell truly believed Tassell
was the man to lead the youth of the GARBC. They continued to apply some "pressure" to convince Tassell of the
importance of this position. On January 15, 1970, with
much reluctance and soul-searching, Dr. Paul finally accepted Dr. Stowell's invitation. On April 5, 1970, Dr. Paul,
Doris, Jann, Jill, and Joe moved to the Chicago area.
There Dr. Paul pioneered a ministry that focused on the
young people of America.

SAYING GOOD-BYE IS HARD TO DO

Good-byes have always been difficult emotional experiences for the Tassells. "Breaking up is hard to do" was the message of one of the popular songs of the day, and for Paul and Doris Tassell saying good-bye to the people of Campus Baptist Church and the city of Ames was one of the hardest things they had ever done. They loved the church, and the church loved them. Charles Cowan, church member and choir director, remembers the "Dr. Paul years" as the "time the church grew the most." He continued, "The church gained new life when Dr. Paul came, and the church was very sad when he left. He was a preacher on his toes, in more ways than one." Yet new challenges lay ahead, so when the tears dried, it was time to put his whole heart into helping to reach the nation's young people. He did, however, take a part of the church with him. His capable secretary, Maxine Nelson, agreed to move to the GARBC office and continued serving as his secretary there.

NATIONAL YOUTH REPRESENTATIVE

As the national youth representative, Paul Tassell remained focused on the pulpit and the pen. "Just let me preach and watch God change the lives of young Americans" was his heart cry. Tassell proved that young minds and hearts could still be stirred with the passionate preaching of God's Word. He also realized that church youth directors and sponsors needed quality youth materials. While still in Ames, at the request of Merle Hull, Tassell had been writing youth material called *Active Christian Teens* (ACT). When he changed positions, he also changed the title of the material to *Wise Active Youth* (WAY). Mary Groe became Dr. Paul's editorial assistant, and without her help the work could not have been done with any sense of satisfaction.

Tassell would preach more than two hundred times a year in camps, youth rallies, junior and senior high school assemblies, and the GARBC national conferences. Tassell and the youth committee enlarged the youth program at the conference from one day to two days and sought to bring assistance and encouragement to youth leaders and young people around the country.

The Tassell children, Jann, Jill, and Joe, have all stated that they had the time of their lives traveling across the country going to all those camps and meeting so many people. They have been in every region of the United States. They have slept in the most modern state-of-the-art accommodations and in the most backward, mosquito-infested, make-a-beeline-to-the-outhouse places one could only dream about. For Dad to preach while on vacation was normal and expected. "Daddy and Mother always made sure they took the time for us to see the national parks, zoos, and monuments. It may have been harder on them hauling us kids around the country, but we loved it."

After three years it became clear to Paul that the position of national youth representative would be difficult to sustain. The state fellowships were waking up to the opportunities for reaching teens for Christ. Many churches were beginning to put on their pastoral staff a full-time youth minister. These youth pastors were doing an excellent job of reaching and teaching the young people. The Bible colleges were adding youth majors as a field of study for ministerial students. State youth programs were organized for rallies and retreats, such as leadership conferences and sports extravaganzas, including basketball, volleyball, softball, and Ping-Pong tournaments. Most churches were using Word of Life, Positive Action for

Christ (Proteens), and Awana materials.

A MINISTRY ENDS

Tassell was not an empire builder. He became more and more convinced that youth ministries could be carried out much more effectively on the state and local levels, with each church utilizing the available materials that best suited them. Dr. Paul and Mary Groe simply could not do the volume of work it would require to compete with Word of Life and Proteens.

The Lord had already prepared a new place for Paul Tassell in the pulpit of Grandview Park Baptist Church in Des Moines, Iowa. He resigned as national youth representative on February 1, 1973, and moved his family to Des Moines on February 18, 1973. Even while pastoring at Grandview Park Baptist Church, Tassell continued to write the youth materials until Regular Baptist Press decided to phase them out. He also continued to do the work necessary to keep Talents For Christ running smoothly. TFC is a nationwide competition of GARBC youth from across the country in various musical and speaking categories. It is held during the annual conference. This task put added pressure on him and his secretary, Velma George, but she never complained. After moving to Des Moines, Dr. Paul made sure to keep all the preaching engagements that he had scheduled before he left the national position.

THE BEST KIND OF SUCCESS

Probably the biggest frustration to a ministry such as national youth representative is how to determine its success apart from dollars and cents. Is something success-

ful just because it sells? Is it considered unsuccessful because it does not sell? Should money be the determining
factor of success? No one would argue the fact that Word
of Life and Awana were successful, and truly they sold a
lot of their materials all around the world. Some would argue that since Dr. Tassell was the first and only national
youth representative and that the *Wise Active Youth* material did not sell all around the world and eventually ended,
Tassell's ministry was just a great experiment that failed;
an idea that really did not work.

But how does one measure new creations in Christ,
changed lives, healed homes, and young people answer-
ing the call of God? How do we calculate success when it
comes to true spirituality, holy living, pure thinking, and
obeying the Word of God? Long after this ministry ended,
Dr. and Mrs. Tassell were sitting in a church pew when
an associate pastor's wife walked up to them, gave them a
big hug and said, "I just wanted to thank you for your ministry in my life when I was a teenager. You spoke at a
youth camp I was attending, and that week I dedicated my
life to the Lord's service." A young man and his wife ap-
proached Dr. Tassell one Sunday morning and said,
"When I was a boy my parents took us to a family camp
where you were the speaker for the week. At the time our
family was in turmoil, but that week my mom and dad re-
dedicated our family to the Lord, and we have been living
for Him since then." Is that not success?

Is not that the best kind of success? The testimonies
of touched lives could go on and on—not only the lives
personally affected by Paul, but all the people ministered
to by the ones called into God's service under Dr. Paul's
ministry. At his retirement and again at his celebration of
fifty years of ministry, people stood in line to relate stories

of how his preaching, camp, and youth ministries had touched their lives in some way.

Author Kathi Hudson wrote, "Success is living in such a way that you are using what God has given you—your intellect, abilities, and energy—to reach the purpose that he intends for your life."[1]

The purpose of Paul Norman Tassell's life was to preach the gospel of Jesus Christ and influence people for the cause of Christ on this earth. Was he successful? We will find the answer to that question in only one place—Heaven.

NOTES

1. Kathi Hudson, quoted by Zuck, 363.

Grandview Park Baptist Church, Des Moines, Iowa

*Success in Scripture is a matter of living out our lives
according to God's expectations and standards
in undaunted routine faithfulness.*

JOSEPH M. STOWELL III

D R. Tassell and his family arrived in Des Moines at an exciting time. In September 1972, Grandview Park Baptist School started with sixty students in kindergarten through the sixth grade. It became obvious that new facilities were needed if the church expected to expand the ministry by adding a grade each year. Tassell led the school board in recommending to the church a large building program at a total cost of $550,000. The twelve deacons, the twelve trustees, and the six members of the school board were unanimous in their decision to present the plans and financing to the church body. Interestingly, the vote to

build the building was 262 "yes" and 2 "no." That was the
exact same vote count to call Tassell as pastor.

The parsonage was next door to the church, so the
Tassell family enjoyed watching the building go up brick
by brick. Joseph Tassell, who was only seven then, remembers secretly climbing on the steel girders at night. Somehow he had failed to mention to his mom and dad that little
secret until years later.

THE CHRISTIAN SCHOOL MINISTRY

Dr. Tassell's predecessor, Harold Scholes, whom Paul
remembers as the greatest song leader in the country, and
the church's youth minister, David Morrison, had prepared
the church body to work together in an admirable unity to
the glory of Christ. The new facilities included a high
school regulation gymnasium, a well-equipped library, fourteen classrooms, science laboratories, and school offices.
The school did prosper, and when Tassell completed his
ministry at Grandview in August 1979, 550 students were
enrolled in grades K–12.

David Keller served as the school administrator, and
later he brought on James Collogan to work with the high
school. Tassell was highly involved in the Christian education of the Des Moines youth. He spoke in chapel at least
twice a week, attended all school board meetings, and assisted Dr. Keller with difficult counseling sessions with students and parents. The church paid off the building debt of
$550,000 in less than twelve years.

BUSY DAYS

Dr. Tassell's ministry as pastor of Grandview Park Baptist Church was busy and blessed by God. With a member-

ship of more than 1,200 people, he had plenty of calls to make, funerals to preside over, weddings to perform, and multiplied hours of sermon preparation. During Tassell's six and a half years as pastor, he baptized 425 converts and took in a total of 650 new members to the church roll. Most of those members went through a membership class taught by Pastor David Morrison.

Doris made the parsonage a place of hospitality. She invited the church members into their home on Sunday evenings for fellowship. The Tassells also visited in many of the homes in Grandview. On one such occasion Dr. Paul went to visit a widow. However, someone mugged him before he could knock on the old widow's door. She promptly pulled him inside the house and called the police, who escorted Dr. Paul back to his car with a warning not to come back to that section of town without an escort.

ON THE AIR

When Paul pastored in Elberton, Galesburg, and Ames, he used a radio ministry as an important part of outreach. Des Moines, Iowa, would be no exception. An excellent soloist, pianist, and organist teamed with Dr. Tassell in a broadcast called *Gospel Views from Grandview.* It was a fifteen-minute program that aired Monday through Friday over three large stations. Grandview Park Baptist Church also broadcast its Sunday-morning worship service. These programs were heard throughout the state of Iowa.

MINISTERING TO COLLEGE KIDS AGAIN

Grandview Park Baptist Church is located just thirteen miles from Faith Baptist Bible College in Ankeny. The president of the college at the time was Dr. David

Nettleton. He had pastored the Grandview church from 1964 to 1967. Tassell and Nettleton were close friends, and the college president asked the Grandview pastor to speak at the college's annual Bible conferences and chapel several times a year. The conference speakers will never forget Thursday evenings after the service when they went to the Nettleton home for coffee and Ruth Nettleton's famous brownies.

THE BLESSING OF GIVING

In 1974, Tassell's pastor friend Dr. Donald Tyler challenged him to institute a stewardship month for the Grandview church. Tassell prayed over the idea and then brought it before the deacons and trustees. After much discussion, the pastor and boards decided to call the Sunday before Thanksgiving "Give a Week's Pay Day." They set a goal of $50,000 to be divided among Faith Baptist Bible College ($25,000), a missions project ($15,000), and building maintenance ($10,000). Tassell urged the congregation to set aside ten percent of their pay every week for ten weeks for the Sunday offering before Thanksgiving. Needless to say, some folks objected to the offering, and Tassell received several anonymous letters asking, "Who do you think you are, telling us how much to give?" On the other hand, the overwhelming majority of the congregation participated joyfully.

The first year the offering totaled $36,500. Three years later the goal of $50,000 in one offering was surpassed. The most joyous part of the stewardship month came at a praise service on the Wednesday night before Thanksgiving. Dr. Tassell asked for testimonies, and there were plenty to go around. One little old lady stood to her feet and testified that she did not know how she would be able to give a week of her Social Security check, but she decided to do it because she loved Jesus. One week before the offering she received a check from the Social Security office due to an error on their records. The check was the exact amount she needed for the offering. Another man stood and said he never thought he could tithe. However, for the last ten weeks he had been putting away ten percent of his week's pay and had not missed a car payment or meal. Another one said, "I have been tithing for years, and this campaign has taught me to double my tithe." God truly gave the increase, and it encouraged Pastor Tassell's heart when he saw the "Give a Week's Pay" offering grow in large amounts while the anonymous letters ceased.

A SURPRISE ENCOUNTER

One beautiful October afternoon Tassell was in his study working on his Sunday sermons when his secretary, Velma George, buzzed him on the intercom. She said in a quiet voice that a strange man had just come in and said he had to talk with the preacher. Tassell told her to show him into the study. When the man came in, Tassell stood looking at a six-foot hulk of a man with a bearded face, bushy sideburns, a big bushy mustache, and hair halfway to his shoulders. He was trembling from head to toe, and Tassell helped him into a chair. The man said, "I am a manager of a Kentucky Fried Chicken. When I got up this morning, I had the overwhelming sensation that I was lost and needed to get saved today. About an hour ago I asked one of my customers if he could tell me how to get saved. My customer told me to come to Grandview Park Baptist

Church on East Thirty-third Street and that someone here would help me." The bearded man began to weep as the conviction of the Holy Spirit was strong in his heart. Tassell opened his Bible and showed him John 3:16 and 1 John 5:12. The man fell to his knees and cried out to Jesus to save him. Tassell prayed, and then the two men stood to their feet and embraced. The man then said, "My wife needs this."

Tassell asked, "Where is your wife?"

He said, "She's out in the car with the baby."

Tassell replied, "Go get her, and my secretary will watch the baby." The man's wife was just as eager to receive Christ as her husband, Tom, had been. In just a few moments she, too, poured her heart out to Christ.

"THE REST OF THE STORY"

Pastor Tassell talked with them a few more minutes, and then he sent them off with the times of the Sunday services. It took Tassell by surprise when Tom and his wife showed up for Sunday School. The beard, sideburns, and mustache were all gone. Tom stood in front of Tassell in a three-piece suit and with a big grin plastered all over his face. He said, "I just thought these kinds of clothes would be more suitable for the Lord's house." His beautiful wife was also dressed modestly and in good taste. It was clearly the work of the Holy Spirit in their hearts, and not some preacher or evangelist. That autumn Tom sold his interest in Kentucky Fried Chicken and enrolled at Faith Baptist Bible College. After graduating there, he went to Grace Theological Seminary in Winona Lake, Indiana. Then he went on to pastor an independent Baptist church in Minnesota.

UNITY AND FELLOWSHIP

There is always something about the will of God that our finite minds just cannot explain. It goes beyond leadership style, charismatic personality, and even individual attitudes. It is . . . well . . . just impossible to fully comprehend why God allows some churches and pastors to come together in a union of grace and harmony and then use those churches in an explosion of God's power that affects the town and even the world. The apostle Paul described it as the "depth of the riches both of the wisdom and knowledge of God! how unsearchable are his judgments, and his ways past finding out! FOR WHO HATH KNOWN THE MIND OF THE LORD?" (Romans 11:33, 34). The key, of course, is easy to know but sometimes difficult to practice, and that is simply the matter of trusting the Lord. The hymnwriter John H. Sammis wrote,

> When we walk with the Lord
> In the light of His Word,
> What a glory He sheds on our way!
> While we do His good will
> He abides with us still,
> And with all who will trust and obey.
>
> Then in fellowship sweet
> We will sit at His feet,
> Or we'll walk by His side in the way;
> What he says we will do,
> Where He sends we will go—
> Never fear, only trust and obey.
>
> Trust and obey—
> For there's no other way
> To be happy in Jesus
> But to trust and obey.

Paul Tassell and Grandview Park Baptist Church fit like ice in lemonade. They melted together in a blend of trust and obedience. The pastor cried, "Just let me preach!" The people echoed, "Just let God use us." When God brings that kind of combination together, He will do things that far surpass our imaginations. In the six and a half years Tassell spent at Grandview Park Baptist Church, hardly a Sunday went by without someone publicly responding to the gospel message or dedicating his or her life to Christ. Dr. Tassell said, "What an incredible joy to pastor such a church!"

A CHANGE IN THE AIR

But the winds of change began to blow again. At the 1978 GARBC Annual Conference, Dr. Stowell announced that he would retire after the 1979 conference. The Council of Eighteen, realizing that the next national representative could possibly lead the GARBC into the next century, had already begun to make their future recommendation to the voting messengers a high priority on their prayer list, praying that God would guide them to the man who could lead the Association to new heights. The man they would choose was Dr. Paul Norman Tassell.

NOTES

Opening Page: Joseph M. Stowell, *Shepherding the Church into the 21st Century* (Wheaton, Ill.: Victor Books, 1994), 79.

National Representative

*In the final analysis, the one quality that all successful
people have is the ability to take on responsibility.*

MICHAEL KORDA

THERE are many types of leaders in this world. Theodore Roosevelt said, "A leader is an average, everyday person who is highly motivated."[1]

Inside Paul Tassell was a drive, a burning determination to serve the Lord with distinction. There was not a bone in his body that had "quit" in it. He had a calling from God to preach the Word of God without hesitation or shame. Tassell was willing to pay whatever price, make any personal sacrifice, and take on any responsibility he believed God wanted him to do. He was not motivated by selfish ambition or personal gain. His goal was not to become the most popular preacher in the land or leave behind some self-regulated legacy. He simply wanted to please God by serving Him with all his heart and strength. Others were recognizing the leadership potential in this man, and it was not long before they called him to national leadership.

Dr. Joseph M. Stowell, whom Dr. Tassell characterized as a "spiritual giant" in his book *Quest for Faithfulness*, had served the General Association of Regular Baptist Churches as its national representative for ten years. Tassell also wrote of Stowell,

> . . . [He] has proved that a man can be a gentleman while being a gladiator. A man can be saintly while being soldierly. A man can be holy without being haughty. A man can be obedient to the Bible without being obnoxious to his brethren. A man can indeed speak the truth in love. He can indeed be a true Baptist without believing that only Baptists are going to Heaven. He can be a true fundamentalist and a true separatist without demanding that every other fundamental separatist dot every *i* and cross every *t* exactly as he does. Dr. Stowell has been a role model for all us preachers.[2]

SEARCHING FOR A SUCCESSOR

At the 1978 GARBC Annual Conference, Dr. Stowell announced his plans to retire after the 1979 conference. "Retire" is an interesting word. To most people it means winters in Florida, golf at least three times a week, and leisurely travel to exotic places in the world. That is not what Dr. Stowell had in mind. Upon leaving the home office of the GARBC, he immediately became the international representative for the Association of Baptists for World Evangelism. He is also, to the very time of this writing, a world-class encourager of young preachers and missionaries. Today his walk may be a little slower, but the fire in his eyes still glows as he continues to serve the Lord.

After the annual conference, the Council of Eighteen formed a special committee to recommend a man to follow Dr. Stowell. The special committee, headed by Dr. G. Arthur Woolsey, sent out letters to the churches of the GARBC asking for their prayers and the names of individual men who might lead the Fellowship. The special committee met, compiled the list of names, and narrowed the list to one man. Dr. Woolsey said, "At the end of the meeting of the special committee, there was one name left on the board, Dr. Paul N. Tassell."

At the Council of Eighteen meetings in December 1978, after a lengthy season of prayer, Dr. Tassell, chairman of the council, was asked to leave the room while the rest of the men deliberated and sought the mind of God. Upon Tassell's return to the room about an hour and a half later, vice chairman John G. Balyo announced that the council had voted to recommend Tassell to be the successor to Dr. Stowell as the national representative of the GARBC. This recommendation would be made at the June conference in Dayton, Ohio.

"BE IT RESOLVED . . ."

At the 1979 conference in Dayton, vice chairman John Balyo, acting as moderator, stood at the podium and announced the recommendation of the Council to the voting messengers. He made his announcement in the form of a motion. A second for the motion came from the floor, and there were no questions. Balyo then called for the vote. It was a simple voice vote. The unity among the messengers was evident when Balyo announced, "The ayes have it," and thunderous applause broke out. John White, secretary of the Council of Eighteen, was overheard to say, "We have just de-Tasselled Iowa." At the Friday evening service, Dr. John White read Resolution #7 titled "Dr. Paul N. Tassell." The last two paragraphs of that resolution stated,

> . . . Therefore be it resolved that we, the messengers of the churches at the 48th Annual Conference of the General Association of Regular Baptist Churches, meeting in Dayton, Ohio, June 25–29, 1979, do commend him [Tassell] to the Grace of God, and shall pray fervently for him that he may have *purity of life, power of leadership, clarity of purpose, compassion of heart, communication skills and convictions consistent with God's Word* and the stated purposes of the GARBC, and,

> Be it further resolved that we will encourage, support and assist him and his family as they assume these new responsibilities [italics added].[3]

THE NEED FOR BIBLICAL MORALITY

No question about it. That was a powerful, desperately needed resolution. As a national leader Dr. Tassell would have to have a pure life. J. Oswald Sanders wrote, "Leadership is influence, the ability of one person to influence others. One man can lead others only to the extent that he can influence them."[4]

As the national representative, Tassell would have incredible influence, especially in the lives of young preachers. He needed to lead by example, and Biblical morality was not an option. It was mandated by God and prayed for by the constituency. He would have to be very careful about what he allowed through his "eye gate" as he traveled the country. He would have to remain totally devoted to his wife, Doris. In a day when every denomination and every association of churches sees many of its leaders fail morally, it was vital that Tassell guard his heart and mind.

We live in a culture that truly celebrates sex, not in a pure sense and certainly not in a Biblical sense. Many men have been taken captive by the Devil's schemes only to ruin a marriage, wreck a home, alienate children, divide a church, and disillusion those under their influence. Most of those same men would be able to say in all honesty that they did not start out with the intention of failing morally and causing the devastation they did on family and flock. However, they would have to admit they let their guard down in their minds long before they acted out with their hands. Dr. Tassell had a mind resolved to remain pure in his thoughts and not give up any ground to the Devil in this area. After fifty years of preaching, Paul Tassell could say he kept his mandate of Biblical morality. He remained true to his Lord, to his wife and children, and to the church.

RESOLVE AND RESPONSIBILITY

That resolve to be faithful enabled him to have power in leadership. Sophocles wrote, "Power shows the man."[5] Chrysostom, one of the early church fathers, said, "Nothing will divide the church so much as the love of power."[6] In a letter to Bishop Mandell Creighton, Lord Acton wrote, "Power corrupts, and absolute power corrupts absolutely."[7]

One of the great observable qualities in Paul Tassell was that he realized that national leadership does not mean power; it means responsibility. For Tassell, responsibility meant hard work and humble service to the 1,600 churches of the GARBC.

HUMBLE SERVICE AND CLEAR PURPOSE

Understanding that national leadership ultimately leads to humble service gave Dr. Tassell clarity of purpose. Article II of the constitution of the GARBC clearly defines the purpose of the GARBC in two sections. Section 1 says,

> To maintain an Association of sovereign, Bible-believing, Christ-honoring Baptist churches; to promote the spirit of evangelism; to advance Regular Baptist educational and missionary enterprises at home and abroad; to raise and maintain a testimony to the truth of the gospel and to the purity of the church; to raise a standard of Biblical separation from worldliness, modernism and apostasy; to emphasize the Biblical teaching that a breakdown of the divinely established lines between Bible believers and apostates is unscriptural and to be a voice repudiating cooperation with movements which attempt to unite true Bible believers and apostates in evangelistic and other cooperative spiritual efforts.[8]

No man can fully understand the scope of that statement, because the Association, and its purpose, is much bigger than any man. However, it is the duty of the national leader to strive to meet that standard and to influence others to do the same. Dr. Tassell believed he could best accomplish this task with powerful preaching, a prolific pen, and propping up pastors with words of encouragement to remain faithful and stay at the work. He knew his purpose and went to work to accomplish his mission with a heart full of compassion, with skillful communication, with convictions based upon the Word of God, and above all else the prayers of the saints.

A NEW MINISTRY, ANOTHER MOVE

The recommendation had been made, the vote taken, the call extended, the answer given, the resolution read, and a new work begun. It was transition time for the Tassell family. Once again it was extremely difficult to say good-bye to another loving church family. When Dr. Tassell went to Grandview Park Baptist Church, he believed he would stay there for the remainder of his ministry. But God had charted a new course for him to follow, one that would take the Tassell family back to the home office in Schaumburg, Illinois. Paul Norman Tassell would spend the next fifteen years of his life as the national representative of the General Association of Regular Baptist Churches.

NOTES

Opening Page: Michael Korda, quoted by John C. Maxwell, *The 21 Indispensable Qualities of a Leader* (Nashville: Thomas Nelson Publishers, 1999), 111.

1. Theodore Roosevelt, quoted by Zuck, 225.
2. Paul N. Tassell, *Quest for Faithfulness* (Schaumburg, Ill: Regular Baptist Press, 1991), 303–04.
3. "Council of Eighteen Minutes—Resolution #7," Dayton, Ohio, June 1979. (Typewritten.)
4. J. Oswald Sanders, *Spiritual Leadership* (Chicago: Moody Press, 1967), 19.
5. Sophocles, quoted by Zuck, 227.
6. Chrysostom, quoted by Zuck, 292.
7. Lord Acton, quoted by Zuck, *292.*
8. Constitution of the GARBC, Article II. Purpose, Section 1.

The GARBC

To be an example believer means that we are indeed, from the very core of our beings, a prototype, a model of what it truly means to believe in Jesus Christ. It is a life not driven by duty to a project, but by devotion to a Person. It is driven by a dynamic, growing relationship with Christ.

J O S E P H   M .   S T O W E L L   I I I

MOODY said, "I took up that word Love, and I do not know how many weeks I spent in studying the passages in which it occurs, till at last I could not help loving people. I had been feeding on love so long that I was anxious to do everybody good I came in contact with. I got full of it. It ran out my fingers. You take up the subject of love in the Bible! You will get so full of it that all you have to do is open your lips, and a flood of the Love of God flows out."[1]

There are many men who know how to run a church. They know theology and deep doctrinal truth. They understand organization, strategic planning, and the ins and outs of technical administration. They can keep the books in order, make sure Sunday School teachers have their materials, visit on Thursday nights, and by Friday night are ready to preach on Sunday. They are the experts and are frequently asked to speak at "How to . . ." workshops in church-growth conferences and seminars. But sometimes a key ingredient, a vital element, seems to be missing. It is an element that appears to be more caught than taught. It is something that expands, grows, cannot fail, and will not quit. When demonstrated in a life, it seems to ooze out through the heart and soul, and it cannot be denied by those it affects. That key ingredient, of course, is love.

AND THE GREATEST OF THESE IS LOVE

Paul Tassell loved the churches and pastors of the GARBC. No one who knows Dr. Tassell in the least bit can genuinely deny that fact. Whether it was a country church of twenty in the boondocks or a church of two thousand in a large metropolitan city, he demonstrated a love for them all. No pastor was insignificant. No church was too small. He believed that becoming the national representative of the GARBC only expanded his ministry to a national and somewhat global level. His desire was to become a pastor to pastors and an encourager to congregations. The one thing that would overshadow any disagreements over philosophy or methods of leadership would be his enthusiastic love for the GARBC shepherds and the flocks under their care.

WHAT ABOUT RADIO?

When Dr. Tassell took the reins of the GARBC, there were many tasks to perform. The first responsibility he tackled was the radio program called *Living Reality.* The program was struggling under some heavy financial problems, and the two people involved in making the program run smoothly, William E. Kuhnle and Grace Matthews, had both retired. Tassell suggested to the Council of Eighteen that if the program could not pay for itself after one year, it should come to an end. At the end of that year *Living Reality* was still running in the red, and the Council voted to let it go.

SIGNIFICANT EVENTS

Some significant events took place in the first years of Dr. Tassell's term as national representative. In 1981, the fiftieth conference of the GARBC took place at Winona Lake, Indiana. That conference generated a book written by Merle R. Hull titled *What a Fellowship!* and a documentary film called *A Living Treasure* on the history of fundamentalism and the GARBC and all aspects of the work at the home office in Schaumburg. These media created an exciting, enthusiastic atmosphere for the conference. The theme that year was "Our Heritage," as the messengers remembered where the Regular Baptists had come from and the brave men who had stood against liberalism.

In 1983, the United States Supreme Court decided against Bob Jones University by denying the school tax-exempt status. At the Niagara Falls conference that same year, the voting messengers of the GARBC passed a resolution declaring that "religious freedom and its exercise no longer exists in unlimited form" in the United States. That resolution was significant because, since that time, Americans have seen an eroding of religious freedoms, especially in the area of expression and utilization of

those freedoms on the part of Bible-believing fundamentalists. In other words, it is good to be a Christian fundamentalist, and it is good to believe in the Bible, and it is
good to believe in Jesus Christ, but it is not good to express those beliefs in public places.

Another significant event took place in 1982 when,
due to failing health, Ruth Ryburn retired. Ruth had been
the secretary for the national representative's office for
thirty-eight years. She was Dr. Tassell's secretary for
three years. He described Ruth Ryburn with the following
words: "She was a friend and fellow laborer. She was com-
petent in her duties, circumspect in her decorum, and
compassionate in her desire to get out the gospel. She
was always loyal to her Lord, to her church, and to her
pastors." Ruth was succeeded by a Nebraska farm girl
named Marianne Baltensperger. Marianne became Dr.
Tassell's secretary in 1982 and served in that position for
the remainder of his tenure as national representative.
Marianne described Dr. Tassell as a superb communica-
tor. "I always knew what I was supposed to do and what
he expected. He ran an efficient office. It was a joy to
work for him and serving the churches. Dr. Tassell was
more than just my boss; he and Doris were also my
friends."

During the 1980s many changes came to the country
and to the GARBC as well. Ronald Wilson Reagan won
the White House with the help of the Moral Majority.
Many Christian conservatives were walking the halls of
Capitol Hill and feeling that the good times had come to
stay. What Christian conservatives failed to realize, however, was that they were really getting a seat at the political table as another special interest group called the "ex-
treme Christian right." That seat entitled them to walk in

some pretty heady and high places, but it also came at a great cost. Now the church, liberal and conservative, would be looked at by the world and its media as just another political action group. No longer would the church be the conscience of the culture. No longer would the church be the voice of God crying out against sin. Now when a pastor stands up against the sins of the nation, he is just another political activist wrapped in religious garb standing under a steeple.

FIGHTING FUNDAMENTALISTS

For some very good reasons many of the pastors of the GARBC, from its inception, could be called "fightin' fundies." They earned this designation because they fought against the liberals. They fought against the modernist agenda. They fought for the inerrancy of the Scriptures and a literal interpretation of the Scriptures. They fought for the impeccability of Jesus Christ. They fought for the substitutionary death of Jesus Christ for the sins of man. They fought for the bodily resurrection of Jesus Christ from the grave. They fought for a literal Heaven and a literal Hell. They fought for a pretribulational Rapture and premillennial return of Christ. When those pastors came out of the liberal Northern Baptist Convention and formed the GARBC, those battles were well defined and the boundary lines well marked. In the '80s and '90s, the lines seemed to get blurred. For the younger generation, those old battles had been won and were over. The mainline denominations, which at one time had held so much power, were dwindling in membership and money and clearly were on the run. That decline resulted in a problematic question: Who does a "fightin' fundie" fight when he's got the liberals in a tailspin? The answer, unfortunately, was himself.

In 1984, the GARBC hit a peak of 1,603 churches in the Fellowship. Around that time it also witnessed the beginning stages of what is now called "postmodernism." Postmodernism is really a throwback to the era of the judges in Israel where "every man did that which was right in his own eyes" (Judges 17:6). Tolerate everything, truth is whatever you want it to be, and be loyal to no one but yourself. Since there are no clear lines, all kinds of skirmishes can flare up anywhere, with challenges on all kinds of issues. In the GARBC those issues ranged from what translation of the Bible should be used, to music, to the role of women in the church, to who should serve on the Council of Eighteen, to the standards on the college campuses, to what churches the board members of those colleges went to, to what color suit and tie the preacher wore in the pulpit. Many of these battles became tests of fellowship in some circles, with the result being, "If you don't do it my way, I'm taking my marbles to some other backyard."

To bring clarity to the maze of different opinions, Dr. Tassell tried to identify this new breed of fighters by calling them "new fundamentalists." But this term in some ways opened the floodgates for more confusion. Dr. Tassell took up his pen and wrote the pastors of the constituency to clarify his meaning of "new fundamentalists." In the second to last paragraph of that letter, he wrote,

> Brethren, there is much work to be done for your Savior. . . . We Regular Baptists need to be busy preaching the Gospel, establishing churches and edifying our congregations. Let us not allow ourselves to be swept into a controversy that is both needless and divisive.[2]

The point was, Let's get back to the real work of the ministry. Those endless little battles over petty things won no one to Christ, built no churches, baptized no new converts, and discipled no believers in the great doctrines of the Bible. All they seemed to do was take up precious time and divide the brethren.

In studying Dr. Paul Norman Tassell's life and ministry, some of his character traits immediately surface. He was a man of integrity, faithfulness, humor, and courage. He did not run away from trouble or problems. He tried to meet them head on, offer suggestions and be part of the solution, and then move forward. At the 1986 conference in Grand Rapids, Michigan, Dr. Tassell stood to give his report as "An Answer, an Exhortation, and a Challenge" to all inside and outside the GARBC who would try to steer it away from its great heritage of Biblical separation to some kind of hyper-separation that was hurting the cause of Christ and the GARBC as a whole. In that report Dr. Tassell said,

> . . . Now let me say something as the National Representative of the GARBC. Let me say something as a rock-ribbed, dyed-in-the-wool separatist. Let me say something as one who has no use for blood-denying, Bible-rejecting, namby-pamby, wishy-washy, white-livered, yellow-backed, thumb-sucking, toe-kissing, liberal preachers. Let me say, God does work through other people in this world besides Regular Baptists. . . . Let's stop training our guns on fellow soldiers and train them on some real enemies who are diametrically opposed to the faith.[3]

Dr. Tassell printed that same report in its entirety in one of the 135 information bulletins he produced during his tenure as national representative. Those bulletins were mailed to more than 2,500 pastors, evangelists, Christian educators, and college administrators.

CHURCH GROWTH CONFERENCES

As a result of that conference and report, the Council of Eighteen and Dr. Tassell formed the Blue Ribbon Committee on Church Planting and Church Growth. That committee held excellent church growth conferences in key locations all across the country from 1986 to 1991. The emphasis was on information, instruction, and inspiration. Dr. Tassell's vision was to get the eyes, minds, and hearts of the leaders and future leaders of the GARBC back where they should be, on fulfilling the Great Commission Jesus Christ gave us before He ascended to Heaven.

WHO'S SITTING ON THE COUNCIL?

The biggest controversy in the Fellowship during Dr. Tassell's years came in 1989, as there was disagreement about who should actually be allowed to serve on the Council of Eighteen. This argument seemed to stem from the approval of two schools, Los Angeles Baptist College (LABC) and Denver Baptist Bible College and Seminary (DBBC&S), and then the subsequent loss of both of those schools. The board of trustees at LABC voted to give the school to Dr. John MacArthur. DBBC&S, plagued with financial problems, merged with Faith Baptist Bible College and Seminary in Ankeny, Iowa. Even though the constitution in Article VII, Section 1, clearly states that the Association cannot create or control any agency, many in the Fellowship blamed the Council of Eighteen for the loss of these schools.

The issue finally came to a head at the Columbus conference in 1989. A motion was made that the Council of Eighteen advise and monitor Western Baptist College about who could be on its full-time faculty, administration, and board. Many in the Association felt that this motion went far beyond the carefully stated boundaries in the constitution. That motion, however, passed with a 669 to 515 vote. A storm was brewing from within, as without a doubt that motion and vote caused division.

At that same meeting, a voting messenger who did not have the blessing of the Council put on "first reading" a proposed amendment to the constitution that would bar any "agency men" (men who work for educational, mission, or service agencies) from serving on the Council of Eighteen. Some in the Fellowship believed that having agency men on the Council was the basis of the problems in the Association in regard to the loss of those two schools and a mission board.

A change to the constitution requires a first reading at an annual conference, a year's wait to vote at the next conference, and then a two-thirds majority vote to pass. The year between the 1989 and 1990 conferences was full of stress and frustration. Dr. Tassell printed his and the Council's view of this issue in the November 1989 *Information Bulletin.*

> ... Be it therefore resolved, That we, the Council of Eighteen of the General Association of Regular Baptist Churches, meeting in session prior to the 58th annual conference in Columbus, Ohio, on June 26–30, 1989, reaffirm our belief in the present composition of the Council of Eighteen as outlined in our Constitution; and
>
> Be it further resolved, That we, the Council of

Eighteen, given the history of our Association, throughout which the messengers have established existing constitutional policy and a satisfaction therewith, express our opposition to the proposed amendment to change the present constitutional composition of the Council of Eighteen.

I agree with the Council of Eighteen. I believe the proposed amendment is *both unnecessary and unwise.*[4]

That Information Bulletin caused no small stir throughout the Fellowship. By the time the messengers met at Niagara Falls in 1990, this issue had been talked about, written about, and probably even preached about from one end of the country to the other. When the vote was taken, the proposed amendment went down in defeat. One thousand one hundred seventy-two (1,172) messengers had voted "no," and seven hundred thirty-six (736) had voted "yes." The constitution remained the same, but there was something different about the GARBC. While the majority breathed a collective sigh of relief, wanting to put this issue behind them and move forward to much more important things, others were angry. They had made up their minds that if this vote went down in defeat, they would pull their churches out and go elsewhere. A few did.

GETTING BACK TO BUSINESS

It was time to get back to the real work of the ministry. There were many miles to travel, many messages to preach, and many ministers to encourage. Serving is what Dr. Tassell did best. At times we all need to be reminded that our Lord Himself "did not come to be ministered unto [served], but to minister [serve]." The very essence of ministry is service. That was what God had called Paul

Tassell to do, and when it came time to pass the baton to his successor, that man would find Dr. Tassell serving.

WONDERFUL COWORKERS IN MINISTRY

Throughout his years as the national representative, Dr. Tassell saw many changes come to the GARBC. He also had the privilege to work with many wonderful, godly men and women. The first eight years he was in the office, the executive editor of Regular Baptist Press was a man who had held that position for thirty-three years, Dr. Merle R. Hull. When Dr. Hull retired in 1987, Dr. Vernon Miller was chosen to succeed Dr. Hull, and he faithfully carried on the work throughout the rest of Dr. Tassell's tenure. Virgil "Mike" Riley had served as the leader for Gospel Literature Services (GLS) for thirteen years, breaking new ground in a vital ministry that serves missionaries all over the world. In 1986, it was time for the Rileys to retire. Dr. Mark Jackson was definitely God's man to take the reins as director of GLS. He took the ministry to new heights, traveling and serving missionaries all around the world. Dr. David Crandall would take the helm of GLS from Dr. Jackson, and in his enthusiastic and energetic hands, he would continue the work of growing that ministry.

SOMETHING AWRY

The winds of change were blowing again in Dr. Tassell's life. He was still traveling, and he was still preaching, and he still had the fire in his bones for the work of the ministry, but something was not quite right. His body seemed to tire quickly, and his voice would grow weaker at the end of his sermons. At first he and Doris thought the rigors and stresses of his schedule

were causing these problems. Then others began to no-
tice his walk was different and his demeanor in the pulpit had become stiff. After speaking at the Wisconsin
Regular Baptist annual conference, the Wisconsin state
representative, James Maxwell, invited Tassell to lunch.
When they had finished eating, Jim pulled his chair a
little closer to the table and said, "May I ask you a very
personal question?"

Dr. Tassell replied, "Sure."

Maxwell asked, "Has anyone ever told you that you
have Parkinson's disease?"

Dr. Tassell sat back and replied, "My wife and I have
suspected something was going awry for some time
now. I shuffle when I walk, my voice gets weaker as I
preach, and I am beset with times of great fatigue." Maxwell related how he had recognized the symptoms right
away due to members in his family with the disease. He
also recommended one of the finest neurologists in
America, whose practice was in the Chicago area.

Dr. Kessler worked Dr. Tassell into her busy schedule the following week. She confirmed Jim Maxwell's diagnosis. Paul Tassell had Parkinson's disease. Dr.
Kessler immediately prescribed medications that would
allow him to have a few more productive years of work.

At the December meetings of the Council of Eighteen in 1993, after fifteen fruitful years of ministry as the
national representative of the GARBC, Dr. Paul Tassell
submitted his plans for resignation. Stress plays a vital
role in the progression of Parkinson's disease, and the
stresses of administrating the Fellowship were too much
for him to continue in that capacity. There were many
tears in that room, but there was also a certainty that
this was God's will for Dr. Tassell and for the GARBC.

T. W. Teall, a council member, accurately penned the feeling in the room with a poem he wrote following the meeting:

ONE UNFORGETTABLE MOMENT
ON THE COUNCIL OF EIGHTEEN

I hesitated to look left or right,
Lest the tear fall from mine eye.
Holy respect and dignity filled the place
As all listened to that big-little guy.

Sure enough a champion, body broke'—
We choked as gently he did cry,
Reading words masterfully penned,
Reflecting fifteen years gone by.

Spokesman, statesman, shepherd, too,
Dynamic alliteration, humor, and wry:
We would never question our great God,
But there are times when you wonder why.

Feeble were our attempts expressing love.
Able communicators challenged in the try
As the magnitude of the moment sunk in,
It was as if the whole Fellowship paused to sigh.

Thank You, Lord, for Your servant named
  Tassell.
Heartfully, hopefully, bind and tie
Our lives with the sweetness of Your grace
And the promise You're always nigh.

The following June at the Seattle conference the Fellowship prepared a wonderful tribute to the couple who had selflessly served them so well for fifteen years. Many men stood and gave testimony of how Dr. Paul had affected their lives and ministries in positive ways. What was truly moving was to hear the words of the young pastors of the Fellowship who said over and over

again, "Thank you, Dr. Tassell, for having time for me, for
encouraging me, and bringing significance to my ministry." What a tremendous legacy as preachers from all
over the country and some even from foreign fields who
had been positively influenced for the cause of Christ by
Paul Norman Tassell thanked the man who had stood in
their corner supporting and encouraging them to keep
the faith and preach God's Word with passion. In a very
emotional moment, with everyone standing, Dr. Paul's
older brother, Al Tassell, came to the pulpit and prayed a
prayer of thanksgiving and praise to God for the years of
service Dr. Paul and Doris had given to the GARBC. As
he prayed, the weeping of the saints could be heard
throughout the auditorium, and when Al said, "Amen," a
spontaneous prolonged and thunderous applause erupted
from the crowd as the Tassells waved good-bye and left
the platform.

Will Rogers wrote, "So live that you wouldn't be
ashamed to sell the family parrot to the town gossip."[5]

In this postmodern age of relative truth and loyalty to
no one but self, Paul Tassell had set an example of Biblical morality, personal holiness, good clean humor, a
strong work ethic, and never-failing love. At age fourteen
he knew God had called him to preach, and that is what
he did for the next fifty years. So what would you hear if
you bought the Tassell family parrot? You would get a
bird that would put his glasses upside down on his nose
and with a sly grin say, "Things are looking up!" or you
would hear the family devotional time at the dinner table,
or you would hear Dr. Paul on the phone encouraging
some young preacher not to give up. No, that family life is
not drama made for TV; it is, instead, the qualities of a life
blessed by God.

NOTES

Opening Page: Joseph M. Stowell, *Shepherding the Church into the 21st Century,* 110.

1. D. L. Moody, quoted by Sweeting, 309.

2. Paul N. Tassell to Pastors of GARBC Churches, January 1982, General Association of Regular Baptist Churches, Schaumburg, Ill.

3. Paul N. Tassell, "An Answer, an Exhortation, and a Challenge" (oral report presented at the GARBC Annual Conference in Grand Rapids, Mich., June 1986). For a written copy, see "An Answer, an Exhortation, and a Challenge," *Information Bulletin* (September 1986).

4. "Who Should Serve on the Council of Eighteen?" *Information Bulletin* (November 1986).

5. Will Rogers, quoted by Sweeting, 220.

Fifty Years a Preacher

Genius is not essential to good preaching but a live man is.

AUSTIN PHELPS

AUGUST 31, 1994, was the last official day Dr. Paul Tassell spent in the home office of the GARBC. For the next three years, he and Doris kept the preaching commitments he had made prior to leaving the national representative's office. They also sold their house in Hoffman Estates, Illinois, and moved to Wisconsin Rapids, Wisconsin, where their daughter Jann and son, Joe, lived with their families. They spent the winters in Winter Haven, Florida, with their daughter Jill. Because of the progression of the Parkinson's disease, they later decided it best to live full-time in Florida. In Winter Haven they bought a comfortable three-bedroom condominium. They became members of Faith Baptist Church in Winter Haven, and in January 2000, the church asked Dr. Tassell to fill the position of staff chaplain.

In John 9, verses 1 to 4, the disciples asked Jesus

about the man born blind. They wondered if the man or
his parents had sinned. Jesus answered their questions by
saying neither the man nor his parents were the cause of
the blindness. The man was born blind to ultimately bring
glory to God. That has been the attitude Dr. Tassell has
displayed since being struck with Parkinson's disease.
Tassell said, "Parkinson's disease is not a punishment for
sins, but an opportunity to bring glory to God." That attitude has encouraged many people across the country
who suffer from incurable diseases. The disease itself at-
tacked Dr. Tassell's voice and gave him what he began to
call a "soft voice." That deterioration made it impossible
for him to preach. Preaching, of course, was Dr. Tassell's
life for fifty years, and though there was the disappoint-
ment of not being able to proclaim the Word of God like
he once had, he now could say with confidence, "For
most of my life I served the Lord talking; now I can certainly continue to serve him with my mouth shut. Our
God is not interested in quick fixes but in quality faith."
One more recent side effect from the disease is that the
tear ducts of Dr. Tassell were loosened. There has been
hardly a church service he can sit through without the
tears flowing down his face. That is especially true when
the cross of Christ is preached.

Doris Tassell learned to face the disease on a daily
basis. She said, "I know that God orders the steps, so it is
my responsibility to make the adjustments and keep on
going, keep on serving the Lord in any way I can." She is
thankful for the small mercies of God, including that her
husband is not in pain and that he is still mobile. The biggest change in their lives is that they are unable to travel
like they used to, as the disease confined them to basi-
cally one location. About a year after the Tassells moved

to Winter Haven, their son, Joe, and his family also made the move to the area, which has enabled the Tassells to spend more time with more of their family and to watch six of their eight grandchildren grow up.

On January 22, 2000, the family celebrated the fiftieth anniversary of Paul Norman Tassell's preaching ministry. The church was decorated with pictures, mementoes, and awards that Tassell had received through the five decades he had been preaching the gospel. Invitations went out about a year in advance, and stacks of mail with pictures and memories from all over the country began to pour in to the Tassell and Osborne houses.

On the day of the celebration, about four hundred people came to congratulate Dr. Paul. The program opened with Mark Smith, the new Sunshine State Regular Baptist state representative, reading a brief history of the life and accomplishments of Dr. Paul Tassell. Next the crowd was treated to a one-time performance of a gospel trio called the Sonshine Boys lip-syncing the words to the song "I'll Have a New Body." The next part of the program was the Tassells' three children giving tributes to their mom and dad for their love, their lives, and their ministry.

A TRIBUTE FROM JANN

Jann Patricia went first and said,

> My name is Jann Patricia Tassell, and I am the oldest child of Paul and Doris Tassell, and as such I must go first; then Jill and Joe can improve on whatever I have done; it has always been this way in our family. Daddy, the way your ministry affected me most is that you have always followed Jesus' example of being a people person. I believe God has blessed you and Mother increas-

ingly over the years because you put Jesus and others in front of your own recognition. I am focusing today on some of the people you introduced into our lives as you ministered to them.

John Cifelli was a man rescued from Skid Row by Jesus Christ with the help of Dr. Paul Tassell in Galesburg, Illinois, when I was three and a half years old. Over the following years he became "Grandpa John" to me and my siblings. When he visited us, we were sure to hear him sweetly singing "How Great Thou Art," accompanied by Daddy's piano. That song is now my favorite song. Grandpa John was an example to us of God's grace in a man's life.

Dr. Merle Hull was a man of great stature, physically and spiritually. I thought of him most, not as the big man of RBP, but as my girlfriend's dad and my dad's good friend. He had a gentle smile and loved his wife and children dearly. Dr. Hull was a precious example to us of God's work in a dedicated life.

Dr. Bob Jones, Sr., who held me when I was a toddler. Kink Allison, who gave me pink peppermints every Sunday in Galesburg. Grandpa Swanson, with his engineer's hat on his white hair. Larry Bleeker from Ames, Iowa, who took souls to Jesus with him from Vietnam. Pat Brannen and Gladys Hawkins, who we thought not only ran RBP but would baby-sit for us in a pinch. Dr. Shipp, with his grand old Chicago church and big, big heart. D. I. Earlandson who, in his eighties, came to visit us at Grandview in Des Moines and battled through a blizzard with you, Daddy, on foot to your office. Uncle Paul Levin and blind Uncle Bob Findley, preaching and singing and twanging at tent meetings. The Csehy Musical Messengers, who filled our home and our churches with heavenly music.

Most of the people I have named have gone on

to Heaven now. With a lot more time I could stand here and name hundreds more people who have impacted the lives of the Tassell family. Some of you are here today. And it is because you, Daddy, Dr. Paul Tassell, have followed in Jesus' way, we have such a great family reunion to long for in Heaven, and you and Mother are my favorite people of all. I love you very much.

A TRIBUTE FROM JILL

Coming next to the platform was Dr. and Mrs. Tassell's second daughter, Jill Priscilla, who said,

I'd like to add to what Jann said. Because of all the people who were introduced to us by our parents, we've had many, many people praying for us through the years. I will always be grateful for that.

One of the defining moments of Dad's ministry that sticks out in my mind took place at the GARBC National Conference in Seattle, Washington, in the '70s. He was in peak form preaching to a packed house, and he made reference to Muhammad Ali and called him "super-lip." The audience in one accord broke into deafening applause. I remember feeling awed and so proud of my father at that moment. Recently, I watched Muhammad Ali on television at the *Sports Illustrated* Awards for Athlete of the Century. Ali also has Parkinson's disease, and it struck me how the disease has affected him and my dad in such similar ways. As I watched them honor Muhammad Ali for his accomplishments in sports, I thought of this day when we would honor Paul Tassell for preaching God's Word. And I thought, what a contrast. Ali's career was all aimed at his own glory. He boasted of being the greatest of all time; but my dad, Paul

Tassell, has spent his life exalting the King of
Kings and the Lord of Lords. He used every
ounce of his energy to serve God and to encourage and challenge people. His accomplishments
will last for eternity. Souls will be in Heaven instead of Hell because of his preaching. It is fit-
ting that we should honor him today. He does
not wish to be exalted, but if the world can proclaim the greatness of someone such as
Muhammad Ali, then certainly the church can
honor a man who has given his life for the gospel of Jesus Christ—

At this point a loud and prolonged ovation erupted from
the crowd. Jill went on to say,

I'm not finished, because while we are honor-
ing Dad, we are giving equal praise and respect
to my mother, Doris Tassell. It is difficult for me
to put into words how I feel about my mom. The
terms that come to my mind are "quiet strength."
She has always been there. I've never heard her
complain—about moving or about Dad being on
the road or about all the work she has done for
all us children through the years—and she has
done a lot of work. Now that I'm a pastor's wife
and have four children of my own, my admiration
for Mother has grown a hundredfold. I strive to
be like her in so many ways. She's quiet, in that
she has never put herself in the forefront, and
she has not sought to advance her own ideas or
projects. She has not lectured us or preached to
us, but only lived a consistent, cultured, Christian
life, an example of a true lady. She is strong in
that her love is unconditional and her loyalty is
unquestionable. She and Dad have accepted
God's will with a practical and positive attitude
that I pray I can emulate in my own life. I thank
God for my wonderful mother.

A TRIBUTE FROM JOE

Finishing up this portion of the program was the Tassells' third child and only son, Joseph Paul. He said,

> Dad, you have been a faithful father to your family, and you taught me to alliterate as well. I thought about alliterating the whole thing, in fact; but I decided not to do that. I thought that might be stealing from you.
>
> My father's intense devotion to ministry never meant a neglect of his family. There are many men who put their careers in front of their family, and their family suffers as a result. We have even seen that with men in the ministry. That has never been true of my father. That has never been true of my mother. They have completely involved us in their ministry every day of our lives. One of the biggest ways, in my opinion, that they have done this is through travel. They did not leave us at home and go on the road preaching in churches and camps and conferences; they took us with them everywhere they went. This traveling has meant a great deal to me through the years. We have become such a close-knit family because of it, and my father taught me by his example as we traveled together what it is to be a godly husband and a godly father. We had the opportunity to visit many historical places and tourist attractions, and we had a lot of fun together. We had the opportunity to do things together as a family that probably most families don't have. And we had the opportunity to see this great land we live in and meet all the people across this nation who call themselves Christians, those who are part of God's family. We didn't see God's family as just a little local church that we were a part of, but we saw that God's family was spread across this whole nation.

I just want to thank you, Dad, for being a real
man. I want to thank you for teaching me to be a
real man. Thank you now for the example that
you are to my boys and helping me to be the
proper example to them so that they can grow up
to be the kind of godly men that they should be.

MORE TRIBUTES

The program continued with a tearful and humorous
tribute to Dr. Paul from his sister Barbara. The Faith Baptist quartet sang a beautiful rendition of "While the Ages
Roll." Next came four tributes from David Gower, executive editor of Regular Baptist Press; David Crandall, director of both Gospel Literature Services and Baptist Builders' Club; Paul Mann, pastor of First Baptist Church,
Pana, Illinois; and Archie Hindal, who served as a deacon
with Tassell at Grandview Park Baptist Church in Des
Moines, Iowa.

David Gower started the tributes with these words:

Dr. Paul, it is our privilege to gather together
today to celebrate your fifty years of preaching. I
think for all of us here who know Dr. Paul, the
name "Paul Tassell" and "preaching" kind of go
together, like pie and ice cream. However, I think
the 10,300 sermons that you've preached over the
last half century certainly provided a lot more nu-
trition and a whole lot less fat than pie and ice
cream did. You know, Paul, you've preached,
you've encouraged preachers, and you've ex-
horted preachers in their preaching. Your preaching heritage has included writing about preaching. I'd just like to share some words from an
article you wrote, "The Preeminence of Preaching," which occurred in the July/August 1990 edi-

tion of *The Baptist Bulletin* [pp. 45, 46]. You said on that occasion, "The preacher is never more useful than when he preaches the Word of God in the power of the Spirit of God to the saints of God. . . . Preachers must major on the preparation and the presentation of Biblical messages. . . . Let's make sure we are preaching the truth and not our opinions. And then let's preach that truth with . . . 'bull-dogmatic' authority. . . . Let's make preaching the preeminent priority in our churches. Let's work hard, brethren, at doing what preachers ought to do. Preach!" So in those words of exhortation, Paul has encouraged all of us who share the Word of God to be students of the Word and proclaimers of the Word.

Paul, we bring you greetings from everyone in the home office. We want you to know we love you, we think of you, and in our Wednesday devotions we often pray for you and Doris. We trust that God will continue to give you opportunity to proclaim His Word as He sees fit.

David Crandall was next on the platform, and, with his usual exuberance and high energy, he paid the following tribute:

I am so very thankful to be here. I just want to say at the very beginning that this family is a great family. I thank the Lord for their thoughtfulness in doing this work to honor this great brother in the Lord Jesus Christ and his faithfulness down through the years of time. So I compliment the family for the work that they have done. I am also grateful for this great crowd of people being able to be here.

One of the things I have always felt bad about is that when I was coming in to the office, Dr. Paul was going out. I was so excited about coming to the office because he has always been one of my heroes, because of his preaching number one; and number two, I always liked his size. He's my size kind of a guy. Normal! Absolutely normal! And then there was Vern Miller—and he's not exactly a giant—so I was so excited to be there *to be with these two normal guys.* And then they leave, and guys like Gower and Greening, who are always hitting their heads on things, are there now.

What a joy to be able to be here and to represent our Fellowship, first of all. I have a letter in my hand that I want to read to you from our current national representative, Brother John Greening, dated January 18,

Dear Dr. Paul,

Praise the Lord for your fifty years of faithfully communicating the Word. You are a model of clarity, passion, and Biblical loyalty in your preaching. You have set a high standard for many years within the GARBC. You have challenged all of us by precept and example to strive for excellence in the pulpit. You are passing on a legacy that will be perpetuated by many lives that you have influenced. May God grant you the strength to continue turning the hearts and minds of your audiences to the Savior.

God bless you and your dear wife, Doris.

With respect,

John Greening
National Representative

David Crandall continued,

That letter represents the more than 1,400 GARBC churches across the United States. I have the joy every weekend to be in a different church; and as I stand before you, this is the truth. In 90 percent of those churches, I can guarantee you there is one question that is always going to be asked me when they find that I am from the home office: "How's Dr. Paul?" You have a great group of people across this nation, Doc, who really love you and respect you greatly. I thank the Lord for that.

I have the joy of standing here personally as well as a pastor who came into the Fellowship under the ministry of Dr. Paul Tassell and his leadership of our national Fellowship. I have the opportunity of standing here as the representative of Gospel Literature Services and Baptist Builders' Club and also as a friend. I thank the Lord for this man of God who has been used so wonderfully down through the years. The Bible puts a high premium on those who finish well. If you don't believe it, go back and read the story of Caleb, who finished so well, crying out, "Give me that mountain." Today we have come to congratulate the two of you for finishing well. We can all look back and say, "Praise God for his ministry."

Now you folks lived in Chicago. You are well aware that in Chicago we have geese. I don't know why we have geese in Chicago, but we have them by the thousands. They leave little visiting cards every time they come to visit us. Engineers have studied the geese because they always fly in a "V" formation. These men have discovered that as geese flap their wings and fly in the "V" formation, the one directly ahead of the other one provides an uplift for the bird behind. Together a flock of geese flying in a "V" formation can go 70 percent farther than they could have gone if they had not been flying in a "V."

Dr. Paul Tassell, as a pastor and as a national representative, a national leader in our Fellowship with your leadership, with your abilities that God has given you, you have given great uplift to thousands who continue on today as a result of

your leadership. God has impacted your ministry
nationally and internationally as well.

Someone has said that fragrance always stays
in the hand of the one who gives the roses. Dr.
Paul, you really smell today. God has allowed you
down through the years to give impact, uplift, and
great encouragement to a lot of us. We stand
here today to salute you and to thank you. God
bless you!

Pastor Paul Mann then brought greetings from First
Baptist Church in Pana, Illinois, and from the Council of
Ten of the Illinois-Missouri Association of Regular Baptist
Churches. He said that the people of their eighty-eight
churches hold Dr. Paul in "high esteem" for his ministry
in their lives across the years. Pastor Mann also said,

I want to thank you today for introducing me to
the ministry. I will never forget the day when Dr.
Tassell rolled into the place where I was employed
and asked me if I would be willing to consider
coming to the staff of Campus Baptist Church to
work with the youth and Christian education. I
said yes to the opportunity, and at that point I was
introduced to the ministry. Dr. Paul also challenged me to the ministry of preaching. Dr.
Tassell said to me on a number of occasions,
"Paul, you've got the choice. You can promote, or
you can preach. I would advise you to preach." He
encouraged me to build a library and to continue
to be a student, to pray, and to be involved in the
lives of people. As a result of that, I have been
blessed. The churches in which I have ministered
have benefited from that kind of ministry.

Dr. and Mrs. Tassell, we count you as good
friends. You have introduced us to the ministry.
You have set a good example for us to finish well,
and by God's grace we shall do that. Thank you,
my dear friend.

Brother Archie Hindal, representing Grandview Park Baptist Church, read a letter of tribute to the Tassells. It stated,

> Dear Dr. Paul Tassell,
>
> What is a preacher? He is a steward and a herald of the mysteries of the manifold grace of God. He knows the Word of God. He knows the people to whom he preaches, and he preaches with a passion and a heart that come from God. From the pen of the apostle Paul we are told that when the preacher proclaims the gospel, it is as if God Himself was making the appeal (2 Corinthians 5:20).
>
> We, the people of Grandview Park Baptist Church, were blessed by God to have had a man of God who preached on his toes. Dr. Paul Tassell was not one to rest on his heels. He knew the urgency of the hour for the hearts of men, women, and children. Many are the homes on the East Side of Des Moines and throughout the area whose families were brought to faith in Jesus Christ through the fire in the pulpit. May the flame never go out!
>
> Dr. Tassell, please accept our congratulations as you celebrate the faithfulness of God throughout fifty years of preaching the gospel.
>
> In His Love,
>
> We, the People of Grandview Park Baptist Church

TRIBUTES FROM THE FLOOR

The next part of the program included a time when anyone from the audience could stand and give a testimony or story about the Tassells' life or ministry. The first one to the microphone was Dr. James T. Jeremiah.

Dr. Jeremiah had been Paul's pastor when he was called
to the ministry. Dr. Jeremiah recalled the following event
that took place in his church when Paul was a teenager:

> I remember Paul Tassell as a young man in my
> church. We had some young people that would
> go up to the balcony and make noise. So one Sun-
> day morning I announced that these young
> people could the next Sunday either sit with their
> parents or come down front and sit with me. That
> whole gang came down and sat with me. And he
> was one of them. Out of that group of young
> people who came to sit with the preacher, several
> of them went out into the service of the Lord.
> That makes me rejoice. We thank God for this
> man and for what he's done and what he's doing
> and how he keeps going. It is a privilege for me
> to be here to celebrate this day with my good
> friend. Now we say congratulations and God
> bless you and continue to use you for the testi-
> mony of the Lord. Amen!

The next man who surprised us by walking to the microphone was Dr. Vernon Miller. Dr. Miller had been
called to the position of executive editor of the Press
while Tassell was national representative. They worked
together for many years. Dr. Miller started his remarks
with these words:

> I'm the other short man. A couple things in my
> life were very important to my ministry. One is,
> God called me. He called me to Himself, and He
> called me to His service. It is a real privilege to
> serve the Lord. Two is that one day Paul called
> me, and we shared together a number of years of
> blessed service for Christ. I counted it a privilege
> to serve with him and to share together I
> saw him step aside in a very sweet spirit. I thank

God for your determination to honor Christ. It
was a great blessing to serve Christ with you.
Thank you so much.

Dan Dark stood next. He pastors Community Baptist
Church in Edwardsburg, Michigan. Dan had been a teenager when Dr. Tassell was pastor at Grandview Park Baptist Church. His church had flown him to Winter Haven
just for the day so that he could share in the celebration
of a man who had meant so much to his life and ministry.
Dan shared some good memories:

> Dr. Tassell, you taught our high school Bible
> class. I don't know how many times you would
> walk into class, turn your glasses upside down,
> and say, "Well, folks, things are looking up." That
> got old, but we had to laugh because you were
> the teacher. I appreciate your fervor and passion
> in teaching the Word of God and the importance
> of the Word of God to us teenagers. I went on to
> Faith Baptist Bible College, and I was just a little
> peon there at the school. However, every time
> Pastor Tassell would come by the college in his
> many travels as the national representative, he
> would stop and talk to me or take me out to lunch
> and make sure I was walking the straight and
> narrow and give me some words of wisdom. He
> really encouraged me in the ministry to preach. I
> wanted to be here today to say thanks and to tell
> you how much we appreciate you.

One of the more heart-touching moments came when
the Tassells' sixteen-year-old grandchild, Jordan, stood
and gave a testimony about his grandpa. Jordan thanked
him for always being there. He said,

> You taught me that whatever I do, do it unto
> the Lord. I want you to know that whatever I do, I
> will do it unto the Lord for the rest of my life.

Thank you for being there for me, and you, too,
Grandma.

Everyone responded, "Amen."

Dr. G. Arthur Woolsey stood next and related the
events that took place when he chaired the search committee for the next national representative. He said he
could remember sitting there going down the list of
twenty-five names they had written on the board. When
they got to Tassell's name, everyone on the committee
felt that Paul Tassell was God's man. Dr. Woolsey said,

> I felt like you would want to know these hap-
> penings on this occasion.

Literally hundreds of letters poured in from all over
the country to commemorate this occasion. Just a sam-
pling is required here to grasp the impact Dr. and Mrs.
Tassell had on so many lives.

Pastor Joseph Bower wrote,

> I well remember your ordination. I was pastor
> of Emmanuel Baptist Church in Toledo when you
> requested ordination. In making the arrangements
> for this important day in your life, I broke all the
> Ohio Regular Baptist rules. The church planned
> for the whole ordination service to be completed
> in one day! One brother wrote, "We do not do it
> this way in Ohio. What will you do if the candidate
> fails the ordination examination?" I responded,
> "He won't." It was a day of blessing which ended
> in one of the most positive recommendations I
> ever witnessed. I thank the Lord for your faithful-
> ness to the Lord and to our fellowship.

Dr. Mark Jackson wrote,

> I am one of the favored few who had the joy of
> working alongside you in the home office of the

GARBC. Thank you for the privilege of the fellowship of those years and the many times we sat together and shared the good days and the tough
ones. The days when you, Vernon, and I labored
together will long be remembered in my experience as a highlight of my ministry. You were always gracious, always generous, and always kind,
and will always be remembered for that and for
your strong convictions.

The grace with which you accepted the path-
way allowed to come your way by the Lord has
not been unnoticed. You have shown the way for
many others. Thank you for being my friend.

Milton Tyrrell, conference coordinator and assistant treasurer at the home office, wrote,

I am privileged not only to have known you at
BJU, but also to have worked with you when you
were the national rep of the GARBC. We've had
many good years serving together in Schaumburg.
Even though it was hard to see you resign, Romans
8:28 has never failed to provide encouragement in
times of trial. You've been an example of the believer to me, Paul, and an inspiration in your preaching.

Virgil Bopp wrote,

Wilma and I have reflected on your pulpit ministry and its profound meaning to us. We are
grateful for these years you have stood without
compromise for the great truths and principles of
Holy Scripture. We are thankful for the straight-
forward leadership style that you gave the Association as well. You were a special encouragement to me when I first put out my book through
RBP. We enjoyed having you in our home, and
found your fellowship a real blessing. Thank you
for all you have contributed to the cause of Christ
and to us personally.

Rudyard Kipling wrote the following lines, which accurately describe Paul Norman Tassell:

> He scarce had need to doff his pride or slough
>   the dross of Earth—
> E'en as he trod that day to God so walked he
>   from his birth,
> In simpleness and gentleness and honour and
>   clean mirth.[1]

For fifty years Paul Tassell had served his Lord simply, energetically, honorably, and cleanly. He preached the gospel of Jesus Christ without shame or hesitation. His whole being was dedicated to impacting boys and girls, teenagers, and adults—young and old—with the good news that Jesus saves. He was our mentor, our example, our colleague, and our friend. He preached on his toes with fire in his heart and graciousness in his eyes. His theology was straight, his vision was clear, his motive was pure, his passion could not be doubted, and his love was unconditional. He was a man with a message from God, and he unwaveringly proclaimed that message loud and clear for half a century.

NOTES

Opening Page: Austin Phelps, quoted by Sweeting, 309.

1. Rudyard Kipling, quoted by Bartlett, 777.

CHAPTER SIXTEEN

Just Let Me Preach

If God calls you to become a minister,
don't stoop to become a king.

CHARLES H. SPURGEON

WHY would an intelligent man spend his entire adult life preaching? That question was posed to Dr. Tassell, and his response was immediate. He answered, "It is a matter of obedience—obedience to the call of God and the Word of God." The call of God gave Tassell purpose, and the Word of God gave him substance. Then he spent the most precious commodity known to man, his time, fulfilling his purpose by proclaiming the truth from God's Word. In Tassell's mind there were never any forks in the road. There were no choices to be made concerning his life's work. God had made it clear to him that he was to be a preacher. In God's Body Paul Tassell would be a voice, and as long as God would allow him, he would use his voice to preach the life-changing truths of God's Word.

With a look back over Paul Tassell's life of ministry,

some things quite obviously stick out to even the casual observer. His preaching is usually the first thing people mention when they remember Paul Tassell. His alliterated outlines never failed to capture the attention of his listeners, and most people in the GARBC either have put their favorite outline to memory or have it written in the flyleaf or margin of their Bibles. Those outlines have traveled the globe, with many young preachers and missionaries continuing to use them.

Another character trait noted about Tassell was his fearless leadership. He did not see too many gray areas in life. There was a right side and a wrong side, and if you were in doubt about which was right or wrong, then you did not pursue the matter until you were sure. Some people would say this philosophy of life is too narrow and that real life is a lot more complicated than that. However, from the Tassell point of view, it made life simpler and much easier to enjoy. Of course, when one limits the number of gray areas in life, then Christian liberties are restricted to some very definable boundaries. But learning to live within those boundaries with love and not making others feel that they have to measure up to your expectations is incredibly freeing. Dr. and Mrs. Tassell mastered that art.

Victor Borge said, "Laughter is the shortest distance between two people."[1] It is true that Paul Tassell loved to laugh and to hear others laugh. His sermons were sprinkled with one-liners that kept listeners' minds from drifting. He would purchase joke books and memorize the lines to stay sharp. When the pressures of life were at their greatest intensity, his humor could diffuse the most problematic situation. His children and grandchildren love to hear him tell a joke and have learned from him how clean humor can make a friend or even clear the air. Now, with the onslaught of Parkinson's disease, Dr. Tassell has not lost his humor and can find a way to laugh at himself, even in the awkward moments this disease brings with it.

Preaching, leadership, and humor are the traits of this man that are easily seen by just about anyone who knows him. But what about the man when he is not on the platform or behind a pulpit? What is he like when he is not chairing a committee or leading the national Fellowship? Is he different behind the spotlight than when he is in front of it? The answer to these questions is the secret to greatness. The secret is consistency. The man one heard preaching from the pulpit was the same man at home. He lived what he preached, not in a gaudy look-at-me way, but simply, gently, and honorably.

Dr. Tassell's ministry has been one of constant encouragement. As the national representative he was the same man in the church of eighty people as he was in the church of eight hundred. He listened attentively to the aged and experienced as well as to the youthful and energetic. He was genuinely interested in each person as an individual and what God was accomplishing through that person's ministry. Over and over again one will hear the testimony of pastors in out-of-the-way places saying, "Dr. Paul always had time for me. He made me feel important." He could make people feel that way because they were important to him. What he did was real, not put on, fake, or phony.

The result of being consistent in his everyday life freed him to genuinely love people. This love was not demonstrated with an outward display of gushy emotion. It was displayed by his kindness, his truthfulness (even

when the truth hurt), and his generosity. He has gener-
ously given to his family, to his churches, to the Fellowship, to mission agencies and missionaries, and to colleges and universities. Because of his consistent giving of
himself, Dr. Paul Tassell has cast long shadows impacting
the lives of people he has never met.

Dr. Paul Norman Tassell's voice is silenced now. In recent years he continued to preach through the ministry of
suffering. He continues to preach through the pages of
the books he wrote. He preaches through the lives of the
people he touched. Praise God! Paul Tassell preaches on!
Let the churches he served and the churches of the
GARBC rise and give praise to God alone for one of His
servants who is finishing well.

> Henceforth there is laid up for me a crown of
> righteousness, which the Lord, the righteous
> judge, shall give me at that day: and not to me
> only, but unto all them also that love his appear-
> ing (2 Timothy 4:8).

NOTES

Opening Page: Charles Haddon Spurgeon, quoted by Zuck, 306.

1. Victor Borge, quoted by Zuck, 221.

Debate over the Virgin Birth of Christ

The following is an article written by Rev. Stanley Borden
of First Baptist Church, Ames, Iowa. It was published
in the "Ames Daily Tribune" on February 6, 1970.

WAS THERE A VIRGIN BIRTH?
Minister Says He Doubts It

. . . The Christian faith begins with the Resurrection, with the breathless realization that he who had been crucified, dead, and buried was alive, that death no longer had the last say, and that this man Jesus, who came from Nazareth, was indeed the Son of God. All that He was and all that he taught and all that he stood for was vindicated by the Empty Tomb. This is the shining central fact of Christian faith. This was what the disciples went out to teach and preach. This is what the early Christians proclaimed they believed when they set themselves apart from all other men with the declaration "Jesus is Lord!" and said, "We will die for this!"

Now the story of the Virgin Birth is not mentioned prior to the Resurrection. Jesus never made any reference to it. Nor is there any record of it in the preaching of the early Church. Obviously, apart from the Resurrection it would be meaningless. The Crucifixion declared that the one born in Bethlehem was mortal like all other men and only that. But the Resurrection introduced another possibility, the possibility of his divinity.

The word of Reconciliation spoken in the Easter event is what gives meaning to the message of Christmas. In terms of time, Christmas comes first. In terms of faith, Easter comes first. How then did the familiar Christmas legends, including the virgin birth, come about?

How and when and where did Jesus of Nazareth become the Son of God? This was the question early Christians had to answer for themselves. And they were pushed by the unbelievers to answer it also. You can't tell us this is the Son of God, or Christ the Lord, unless you tell us how it came about. Certainly they must have had that thrown at them many times.

THEOLOGICAL ROOTS

In the New Testament we can trace three answers which emerged to these questions. The first: Jesus became the Son of God at his Baptism; this is when the Holy Spirit came upon him. The second said: Jesus became the Son of God by virtue of his being born of the Virgin Mary. And the third said: Jesus was the Son of God from the beginning of time; there never was a time when he wasn't. These three strands of thought appear alongside each other in the Bible and note well that they all point overwhelmingly to the same conclusion: that Jesus was the Son of God.

The first theory that developed was the so-called Adoptionist theory, the idea that God selected the fine, upright young man, Jesus of Nazareth, and set his seal upon him, adopting him through baptism to be His Son. . . .

But that theory has some difficulties. Was Jesus a sinful man before his baptism and did the baptism wipe out his sin? That's sort of a troublesome thought. Or if he was sinless before his baptism was he not then the Son of God before his baptism? And so they kept pushing the idea back and the second theory developed that his Incarnation must have dated from his very birth. He was born sinless and never sinned. He was born the Son of God. And many found this the most satisfying answer to their question. The story of his birth from a virgin fitted in with this. . . .

Once they had started pushing the Incarnation back, however, they could hardly stop there. If this man was the Son of God and the full revelation of God, where had God's revealing presence been before that? Did the Redeemer just start up from nothing at the moment of Jesus' conception by the Holy Spirit? Was the reality which they knew in the Risen Christ unrelated to God's act in Creation and not present in any way in Moses and the prophets? And if it was the same reality, then how could it have just begun with Mary?

So it was that a third theory developed which was built around the idea of the preexistence of Christ, that he was present with God from the beginning of the world and became a human being in the life of Jesus of Nazareth. This is the theory which reaches its loudest expression in the first chapter of John. "In the beginning was the Word, and the Word was with God, and the Word was God." Then later, "And he became flesh and dwelt among us full of grace and truth." John not only makes no reference to the Virgin Birth, but his glorious concept of the Incarnation is no way dependent upon the Virgin Birth!

LITERARY ROOTS

Where did the birth legends come from? We have talked about the theological roots. What are the literary roots? Some Bible critics point to the strong parallels in pagan literature and mythology, and treat these as if they were taken over from such sources and just cleaned up enough to suit their new purposes. Yes, these stories of miraculous births or conceptions do exist in ancient lore, but the time has passed when anyone sees any direct connection between these and the Christmas stories.

The parallel myths in pagan literature almost always stress an immoral and licentious sex act between the sons of the gods and the daughters of men. They have none of the sweetness and purity of the New Testament account. The differences are so profound that they nullify the slight similarities which exist. If they have any relationship at all, it is simply to establish the fact that in those times a frame of mind existed which was open to this type of account in the stories of the origins of the gods.

The legend of the Virgin Birth as we have it in the New Testament undoubtedly has its origins in the Prophecy of Isaiah concerning the Messiah. Matthew clearly associates the two: "All this took place to fulfill what the Lord had spoken by the prophet: Behold a virgin shall conceive and bear a son, and his name shall be called Emmanuel" (Matthew 1:22, 23; Isaiah 7:14). Evidently, stories already existed about the birth of Jesus; and these were molded and adapted to harmonize with Matthew's reading of this prophecy. After all, we know that one of Matthew's chief goals in his gospel was to show his Jewish readers how many events in the life of Jesus could be considered as fulfillment of the expectations of their own Jewish scripture.

MISREADING

Evidently, Matthew misread ancient scripture for re-member the passage he was quoting was 800 years old in his day, and he had none of the aids of modern literary scholarship to assist him. We now know that the Isaiah verse does not refer to a virgin in the technical sense in which we use that word. In the Hebrew, the word used is "almah." It normally meant simply "young woman." How-ever, Matthew was familiar with the Greek Bible known as the Septuagint, and in this a Greek word is used, transla-tion meaning virgin, although even this word is occasion-ally used of a girl who is no longer a virgin. But Matthew ties the event to this prophecy because he interpreted in the narrower sense so that it could easily mean that the child had no human father.

From that point the story weaves together many ele-ments, some of them quite fanciful, some of them quite likely having historical roots. The resulting story is one that is simple, beautiful and profound. It glows with the warmth and adoration of those who knew Jesus Christ as Lord and Savior, and it stands as a memorable testimony to their faith. There is no evidence that it was a cause or a reason for their faith.

In other words, no one believed in Jesus as Lord be-cause he was born of a virgin. There isn't the slightest hint of this in the New Testament. But many who believed in Jesus as Lord accepted these legendary accounts of his birth. And it is plausible to do so. Once a person has been confronted with the reality of the life of God in the man Jesus Christ, and has accepted the fact of God's power working mightily in this particular person, it is not hard to believe that his birth also should have witnessed to the working of God. The God who healed the sick and raised the dead could have brought to pass the events described regarding Jesus' birth. It could have happened.

OTHER EVIDENCE

But the literary evidence strongly suggests that it did not. In Matthew the angel of the Lord appears to Joseph to reassure him about his wife's expected child. The account as we know says "she will bear a son and you shall call his name Jesus." Later it says "He took his wife but knew her not until she had borne a son." Now some of the ancient Syriac versions read differently at this point.

The message to Joseph is that Mary will bear him a son, and the later passage also says "and when she had borne him a son." Evidently, in these early versions of the birth story Joseph was the natural father of Jesus; but somewhere along the line, this reading was dropped in favor of the one which suggests Mary's virginity. This was part of the process of harmonizing the various concepts of when Jesus became the Son of God.

There is also the interesting confusion as to the relationship between Mary and Joseph. In Matthew 1:13 Mary is described as being "betrothed" to Joseph, indicating that they were formally engaged to be married. Yet two verses later she is referred to as his "wife" and the Hebrews normally did not use that term until after the man took his bride to his home and the marriage was consummated. Also, his traveling with her to be registered would indicate that they were husband and wife, not an engaged couple. The idea that they were only betrothed was evidently introduced to protect the growing legend of the Virgin Birth.

There are other reasons besides literary ones for questioning the Virgin Birth. We have already mentioned that the two greatest evangelists John and Paul seem never to have heard of it. If it had been a cause for their belief in Jesus' divinity, they certainly would have shared this startling fact. And if it was considered by either of them to be a matter of faith essential to salvation, then certainly they would have made that very clear to their converts. But they did not.

TWO OTHER FACTORS

There are two other factors we have to make clear regarding the Virgin Birth. An outdated view of human sexuality treats all intercourse as sinful and, therefore, by implication no child conceived through the normal act of husband-wife relations could be the Son of God. If sex is sin, then the Son of God would have had to be conceived some other way.

Closely related is the misreading of original sin, as if it was something carried on and inherited in the normal process of human conception and birth. If Jesus was sinless then he could not have had a human father, or he would have inherited this trait. Then of course, the question is raised: what about inheriting sin from his mother? It was this dilemma which lead the Catholic Church to develop the Doctrine of the Immaculate Conception of Mary.

Mary had to be sinless so that Jesus could be free from this taint. So if you start tracing Jesus' sinlessness from his virgin birth, your logic drives you relentlessly into such totally unscriptural conclusions as the Immaculate Conception. It also drives you to the Catholic doctrine of the perpetual virginity of Mary thus denying any real brothers and sisters to Jesus.

Original sin is not something in our genes, but it is that bent of the will to exercise that freedom by defying God. It is [a] stamp on our humanity but not a product of our inheritance.

Belief in the Virgin Birth today is primarily a by-product of Fundamentalism. That point of view which insists on verbal inspiration and absolute literalism simply starts from a promise which makes it impossible to treat the scriptures the way they were really written or to interpret them intelligently in light of the early Church. Such people believe in the Virgin Birth not because it is essential to salvation but because it is essential to their strange notion of the Bible.

Their literalism is [a] balloon which if pricked at any point it would burst. Therefore, they cannot entertain any literary criticism or theological challenge to traditional doctrines no matter how sincere and well founded it might be. I am sure you realize well that it is this kind of blind and irrational dogmatism which has driven 80 percent of today's college students away from the Church entirely and made it impossible for them to hear Christ's claim on their lives.

But the claims of Christ are not dependent upon the Virgin Birth. His deity, his lordship, his redemptive reality in our lives rests upon firmer ground for sure.

❖   ❖   ❖

Having read that sermon in the paper, Tassell could not sit still until he had set the record straight. The liberal would not be allowed to spew heresy without a strong and convincing rebuttal of his false views. Tassell went to work and preached a message that was printed in the same paper one week later on February 13, 1970. The message is as follows:

MINISTER PRESENTS OTHER SIDE OF ARGUMENT ABOUT VIRGIN BIRTH

The Virgin Birth of Jesus Christ is clearly presented in the Bible. Both Matthew and Luke carefully relate the events preceding the birth of Christ. Both make it very clear that Mary was a virgin at the time of Christ's birth. It is interesting that Luke, who gives the most detailed account of the virgin birth, was a physician. It is also noteworthy that Luke was a traveling companion of the Apostle Paul; so for a liberal writer to say of the virgin birth "John and Paul seem never to have heard of it" is to be less than astute.

All the great branches of Christendom have taught the validity of the virgin birth since the first century. Roman Catholicism, Greek Orthodoxy, Protestantism's great creeds—all have faithfully and factually taught the Scriptural basis and necessity for the virgin birth of Christ. From Augustine to Martin Luther, from John Wesley of Methodism to Benjamin Warfield of Presbyterianism—all of the worthy scholars and faithful proponents of Christianity have given witness to the overwhelming evidence of authentic Scriptural history that Jesus was indeed the virgin-born son of Mary.

MISREPRESENTATIVE

Words such as "legends," "theory," "myths," "legendary accounts," "the growing legend of the Virgin Birth" are grossly misrepresentative of the carefully documented, historically accurate writings of Matthew and Luke.

The liberal writer tries to make the reader believe that the fundamentalist bases his entire case for the virgin birth on the translation of the Hebrew word "almah" in Isaiah 7:14. However, the case for the virgin birth is built on a much more solid foundation than just this one word. Matthew does, however, translate "almah" virgin: but he does far more than that! He says very clearly: "Now the birth of Jesus Christ was on this wise: When as his mother Mary was espoused to Joseph, before they came together, she was found with child of the Holy Ghost" (Matthew 1:13).

Matthew also says: "Then Joseph being raised from sleep did as the angel of the Lord had bidden him, and took unto him his wife: And knew her not till she had brought forth her firstborn son; and he called his name JESUS" (Matthew 1:25).

EXPLAINS

Matthew was careful to explain just exactly how Mary came to be a mother without the means of sexual intercourse. To question the virgin birth is to question Matthew's integrity as an historian, to say nothing of his integrity as a disciple of Jesus Christ. The great Southern Baptist scholar, John A. Broadus, has written: "This Hebrew word is almah. Another word, bethula, generally means virgin, but in Joel 1:8 is clearly applied to a young wife. If such an instance had been found for almah, it would have been claimed as triumphant proof that virgin is not here a proper translation. The result seems to be that almah certainly does not prove a virgin birth but fully admits of that sense, which Matthew confirms."

In other words, the translation of almah depended upon the context in which it was used. Every Hebrew scholar worthy of the name knows this. It is obvious from an objective reading of Matthew's narrative that he was talking about a woman who still retained her virginity and whose child was to be conceived by the Holy Ghost.

The liberal writer failed to refer to Luke's extensive account of the virgin birth. The fundamentalist's case is greatly bolstered by Luke's account in which he says, "And in the sixth month the angel Gabriel was sent from God unto a city of Galilee, named Nazareth, to a virgin espoused to a man whose name was Joseph, of the house of David; and the virgin's name was Mary" (Luke 1:26, 27).

Twice Luke refers to Mary as a "virgin," and he was not translating Isaiah here; he was simply reporting factual history. No doubt, Luke's traveling companion, the Apostle Paul, had Luke's account in mind when he wrote, "But when the fulness of time was come, God sent forth His Son, made of a woman, made under the law" (Galatians 4:4, 5). I would much rather place my faith in first-century men like Matthew, Luke and Paul than in the speculations of biased twentieth-century "doubting Thomases."

HISTORIAN

The eminent archaeologist, Sir William Ramsey, has written, "Luke is an historian of first rank; not merely are his statements of fact trustworthy; he is possessed of the true historic sense; he seizes important and critical events and shows their true nature at greater length, while he touches lightly or omits entirely much that was valueless for his purpose. In short, this author should be placed along with the very greatest of historians."

Dr. Otto Piper says, "Wherever modern scholarship has been able to check up on the accuracy of Luke's words, the judgment has been unanimous; he is one of the finest and ablest historians in the ancient world." And Luke's writings, Luke and Acts, comprise more than one-fourth, almost two-sevenths, of the New Testament, and Luke says dogmatically that Jesus was born of the virgin Mary. Luke is not a fundamentalist "balloon"; he is a bed-rock of authority!

The great Congregational scholar, Dr. O. J. Brown, who holds the Th.M. from Harvard Divinity School and a Ph.D. in history from Harvard's Graduate School of Arts and Sciences and who today is the theological secretary of the International Fellowship of Evangelical Students in Lausanne, Switzerland, says, "The historic Christian con-viction, from the earliest times, has been that God does authenticate his claims by evidence (cf. Luke 1:3, 4; John 20:30, 31). One could really say that this is what the Bible is all about. We must be content with two rather prag-matic statements of fact: (1) On the basis of the best avail-able evidence, it is easier to believe in the complete trust-worthiness of the Bible today than at any time in the past century. (2) People who claim to be finding errors on sci-entific grounds almost always demonstrate a degree of preconceived opinion which makes their objectivity doubtful."

GREATEST SCHOLAR

With reference to the validity of Matthew's account of the virgin birth, the greatest New Testament Greek scholar of the twentieth century, Dr. A. T. Robertson, says: "It is remarkable that the oldest scrap of papyrus of any portion of the New Testament contains the ordinary Greek text of Matthew 1. The papyrus (P) is at the University of Pennsylvania and belongs to the third century A.D. So far as the manuscript evidence goes, the Virgin Birth narrative in Matthew and in Luke cannot be seriously challenged."

Dr. Robertson also asserts, "The virgin birth is the only intelligible explanation of the Incarnation ever offered. Both Paul and John picture Christ as existing before his incarnation. When we get rid of the Incarnation, we have only a naturalistic social gospel with no converting and transforming power for sinful men. If we believe in a real incarnation of Christ, we cannot logically object to the Virgin Birth on the ground of the supernatural feature in it. If we take Joseph to be the actual father of Jesus, we are compelled to be illogical if we hold to the deity of Jesus."

The Roman Catholic Church, the Greek Orthodox Church, the great Protestant creeds are on solid ground, Scripturally and historically, when they maintain the validity and authenticity of the virgin birth. The integrity of the Bible is at stake when we consider the authenticity of the virgin birth. If the Bible cannot be trusted to speak truthfully and accurately concerning Jesus' birth, how can we be sure the Bible is accurate when it speaks of Christ's death and resurrection? The same Bible which speaks of the virgin birth tells also of salvation from sin through faith in the virgin-born son of God. How could we trust our eternal souls to the Bible's message of salvation if we cannot trust the authors of the Bible to tell us the truth about Jesus' birth?

REJECTION

When you reject the validity of the virgin birth, you reject the authenticity of Scriptural authorship and authority. I have done extensive work in the field of textual criticism. I have taught New Testament Greek at the college level, and I speak from first-hand knowledge when I testify to faith in the trustworthiness of the Bible. My faith is not blind; it is built on great and overwhelming evidence. The Apostle Peter wrote, "We have not followed cunningly devised fables, when we made known unto you the power and coming of our Lord Jesus Christ, but were eyewitnesses of his majesty" (II Peter 1:16).

The Biblical message of the Gospel of Christ is attracting tens of thousands of college students across the world. Campus Bible Fellowship, the Navigators, Campus Crusade for Christ, Word of Life Fellowship—all of these groups are seeing thousands of college students turn from the institutional, liberal church establishment to the Biblical message of the Gospel which offers salvation, not speculation; and faith, not fables.

Outlines
of Best-Loved Sermons
Preached by Paul Norman Tassell

SERMONS FROM GENESIS

The Great Decrees from the Great Creator
(Genesis 1:1–31)

   I. The Division (1:1–5)
  II. The Dome (1:6–8)
 III. The Dressing (1:9–13)
 IV. The Diadems (1:14–19)
  V. The Deep (1:20–23)
 VI. The Dominion (1:24–31)
     A. God Made
     B. God Mandated
VII. The Declaration "Very Good"

The First Wedding (Genesis 2:1–25)

   I. The Dust (2:1–7)
  II. The Delight (2:8–14)
 III. The Dressing (2:15)
 IV. The Discipline (2:16, 17)
  V. The Designations (2:19, 20)
 VI. The Deficiency (2:18)
VII. The Dame (2:21–25)

The Awful Fall (Genesis 3:1–24)

   I. The Denial (3:1–5)
  II. The Desire (3:6)
 III. The Deception (3:6)
 IV. The Disobedience (3:6; cf. 1 Timothy 2:14)
  V. The Dread (3:7–11)
 VI. The Dying (3:12–19)
VII. The Driving (3:20–24)
     A. The Provision by God
     B. The Pity of God
     C. The Protection

The First Murder (Genesis 4:1–26)

   I. The Darlings (4:1, 2)
  II. The Devotions (4:3–5)
 III. The Dejection (4:5, 6)
 IV. The Danger (4:7)
  V. The Deed (4:8)
 VI. The Dishonor (4:9–15)
VII. The Descendant (4:25, 26; cf. Luke 3:38)

The Original Obituary (Genesis 5:1–32)

    I. The Dirge
    II. The Dedication ("after Methuselah")
    III. The Daring
    IV. The Deliverance ("God took him")
    V. The Disappointment ("969")
    VI. The Discernment
    VII. The Descendants

Dr. Tassell preached the following "I Love the Lord Because . . ." series in many Bible conferences across the country. This outline is from Isaiah 59; Psalm 116; John 8; and Ephesians 2.

I Love the Lord Because . . .

    I. He Listens to me; therefore, I will Pray.
    II. He Looses me; therefore, I will Prevail.
    III. He Lifts me; therefore, I will Progress.
    IV. He Levels with me; therefore, I will Perceive.
    V. He Loads me; therefore, I will Prosper.
    VI. He "Loyalizes" me; therefore, I will Praise Him.
    VII. He Labors with me; therefore, I will Persevere.
    VIII. He Lives for me; therefore, I will be a Priest.
    IX. He Leads me; therefore, I will Pursue Him.
    X. He Lightens me; therefore, I will Proclaim His Message.
    XI. He Laves me; therefore, I will Purge Myself.
    XII. He Longs for me; therefore, I will Prepare to Meet Him.
    XIII. He Links me; therefore, I will Participate.
    XIV. He Lodges with me; therefore, I will Produce.
    XV. He Loves me; therefore, I will Please Him.

Dr. Tassell preached the following outline in a series of four messages at Faith Baptist Bible College's February 1991 Bible conference. The text is Romans 6:1–17.

I Will Say No to Sin Because . . .

I. My sin displeases God.
II. My sin disappoints my neighbor.
III. My sin devastates my ministry.
IV. My sin deprives me of joy.
V. My sin denies the authority of God's Word in my life.
VI. My sin darkens my understanding of God's will for my life.
VII. My sin desensitizes me to sin's terrible nature.
VIII. My sin deters my prayer life.
IX. My sin directs others to sin like me.
X. My sin diminishes my fruitfulness.
XI. My sin dishonors my local church.
XII. My sin divides my loyalties and energies.
XIII. My sin distorts my thinking.
XIV. My sin devours my reward.
XV. My sin destroys some.
XVI. My sin delights the Devil.

With the diagnosis of Parkinson's disease, Dr. Tassell preached this message titled "Heaven: The Healing Haven." It is from Revelation 21:1–5 and Revelation 22.

Heaven: The Healing Haven

I. Broken Hearts will be Healed in Heaven.
II. Bewildered Heads will be Healed in Heaven.
III. Benumbed Hands will be Healed in Heaven.

Dr. Tassell preached the following outline in a four-part series titled "Amazing Grace." His text was Titus 2.

Amazing Grace

    I. Saving Grace
   II. Sanctifying Grace
  III. Serving Grace
  IV. Schooling Grace
   V. Suffering Grace
  VI. Separating (Dying) Grace
 VII. Stabilizing Grace
VIII. Sacrificing Grace
  IX. Stimulating Grace
   X. Stretching Grace
  XI. Sobering Grace
 XII. Styling Grace

Dr. Tassell preached the following message outline at the Sixth Fundamental Baptist Congress of North America. His text was Acts 1:9–11.

The Second Coming of Christ

  I. A Resurrected Man is Coming
    A. A Corporal Resurrection
    B. A Cardinal Resurrection
    C. A Characteristic Resurrection
 II. A Righteous Man Is Coming
    A. A Rebellious World
    B. A Righteous Man
    C. A Revealing Judgment
III. A Regal Man Is Coming
    A. A Regal Priesthood
    B. A Regal Place
    C. A Regal Power
    D. A Regal Person